To Lor

Isn't it wonderful to be loved at CBC?!

I Am Loved
at Community
Bible Church

Enjoy!

Love,

Sandi

Dr. Sandi Adams Hutcheson

ISBN: 1500693286
ISBN 13: 9781500693282

Dedication:

To Horace and Glennis Adams and Buford and Babs Adams, the founding fathers and mothers of this ministry.

To Beau and Kim Adams, who continue the work with huge amounts of love and grace.

And to everyone who has ever greeted a visitor, changed a diaper, taught a Sunday school class, or in any way volunteered your time or given financially to the work of the Atlanta Youth Ranch, Community Bible Church, or Community Christian School. You are the reason this ministry is celebrating its 50th anniversary.

Introduction

*Here's the church, here's the steeple, open the doors
and see all the people.*

Multitudes of people have come through the doors of Community Bible Church since the day they opened for the first time in 1969. I was two years old and lived inside those doors along with my dad and mom and little brother.

I played hide and seek in the darkened buildings when I was little. I was the first student of Community Christian School and one of its early graduates. I worked at the church for nearly twenty years.

I remember the Easter Bunny getting out of that helicopter in 1973. I can still see all those rain-soaked barbeque chicken dinners during the ill-fated Bicentennial celebration. I sat through more of my dad's sermons than anyone else except my mother.

In other words, what you're about to read is a work by the ultimate insider. Thorough research is necessary for telling a good story, and if pressed to describe the research I've done for this book in church terms, I'd have to call it a baptism by total immersion.

I would love to claim that this work is completely objective. I've interviewed many people in writing this history of Community Bible Church, getting the stories from their perspective. But I'm also telling this history the way I remember it, which means readers must take into account the bias of a girl who always has and always will love this place.

One other thing: my training in journalism and nonfiction writing taught me to use the last name rather than the first in referring to people, but it was too cumbersome and confusing in this book because there are so many Adams. Please forgive me for ignoring that rule.

Sandi Adams Hutcheson
April 2014

I Love to Tell the Story

I love to tell the story; it did so much for me,
And that is just the reason I tell it now to thee[1]

On a sweltering August morning in 1984, a group of ten men met in a church auditorium in Atlanta, Georgia. After coffee and doughnuts and a brief exhortation from the church pastor, the meeting was turned over to a nuclear physicist, who gave careful instructions to those gathered. The group included two preachers, an engineer, a high school principal, a Delta Airlines mechanic, and an accountant. When the scientist finished speaking, the men donned hazmat suits and went to work.

Two decades before, on December 17, 1963, President Lyndon B. Johnson had signed into law the Clean Air Act, legislation designed to control air pollution. The law was amended in 1970 to provide national emission standards for permissible levels of hazardous air pollutants. In 1971, the Environmental Protection Agency (EPA) was created to implement the requirements of the 1970 version of the Clean Air Act, which required the Agency to list air pollutants that were potentially dangerous to human health. Asbestos made that initial list, and in April 1973, the EPA set national emission standards for asbestos. Then, in 1977, an amendment to the Clean Air Act

---

1 Words by A. Catherine Hankey

prohibited the use of spray-on insulations containing more than one percent asbestos and mandated the renovation of "any institutional, commercial or industrial" building to be in compliance with asbestos regulations.

On June 21, 1976, the EPA delegated to the Georgia Environmental Protection Division (EPD) the authority to enforce "all aspects of regulations pertaining to the use, removal, and disposal of friable asbestos-containing materials from . . . sites."[2]

Simply stated, the EPA gave Georgia's EPD the responsibility of determining the exact danger posed by the presence of asbestos in Georgia's public and commercial buildings and thereby mandating its removal.

In the spring of 1984, the EPD tested the popcorn-style spray-on ceiling of Clayton Community Church's first auditorium in Morrow, Georgia, and determined that it had the potential to release cancer-causing fibers into the air. Although it would be two years before the Asbestos Hazard Emergency Response Act (AHERA, 1986) was passed requiring schools and public and commercial buildings to remove hazardous asbestos, the Georgia EPD ordered the church to remove the asbestos from that auditorium immediately or stop using the facility for public meetings.

Estimates for the removal by a professional company came in at nearly $50,000, money the church simply did not have. But Dr. Ed Sturcken, a member of the church who was a nuclear physicist specializing in hazardous materials cleanup at the Savannah River Site near Augusta, Georgia, suggested they could do the work themselves. He assembled the necessary suits, equipment, and masks -- everything needed to perform the task. Another

---

2 From a document titled "Notification Procedures for Friable Asbestos-Containing Materials" in Community Bible Church records.

member of the church, Bill Barton, owned a hazardous waste removal company, and he provided an appropriate disposal unit. The men who gathered on that hot summer morning were members of the church who volunteered to help remove the asbestos from that ceiling.

The volunteers put on the hazmat suits consisting of Tyvek coveralls, hoods, and shoe covers. Masking tape was used to seal around wrists and ankles. They proceeded to remove the asbestos from the ceiling by spraying it with water, scraping it off, putting it in plastic sacks, and throwing it into the dumpster that had been provided for the cleanup operation.

The air conditioning had to be turned off during the entire process because it would blow the dangerous particles around. "It felt like a zillion degrees inside those suits," Buford Adams, the church's pastor, remembers.

Two hours after they'd begun the work, an official from the EPD showed up. He had a startled look on his face. "What in the world are you doing?"

"We're getting rid of the asbestos," Sturcken answered.

"You can't do that. You have to be certified, and you must provide a ten-day notification to the EPD before doing the work," the man insisted, adding, "This is dangerous."

"Are we doing it wrong?" Sturcken asked.

The man admitted that they were doing it correctly. And when they produced a letter from the Department of Natural Resources granting Barton Environmental a waiver from the ten-day notification requirement, the man shrugged his shoulders and left. Weeks later, the cleanup passed inspection, and the church never heard from the EPD, at least on that issue, again.

Without realizing it, that EPD official had hit upon one of the cornerstones of the church's success. From its inception in the late

1960s, the church and its leadership have consistently done things differently. Not wrong, but certainly not the way most churches did things.

And it was that way from the very beginning.

Faith of Our Fathers

Faith of our fathers, we will strive
To win all nations unto thee
And through the truth that comes from God
Mankind shall then indeed be free[3]

The end of World War Two brought hope to America. The country had suffered for nearly two decades, starting with the Great Depression and then the Great War. Defeating the Axis powers and putting a stop to the horrors that had been perpetrated upon millions of innocent people allowed Americans to feel good about themselves and the future once again. Perhaps it was idealism, the unassailable belief that good overcomes evil when people fight for what is right, or maybe it was that after many years of scarcity and fear, Americans needed to replenish their spiritual wells. Whatever the reason, at the same time young soldiers returned home from the war and the Baby Boom started, church attendance in the United States soared.

One of those young soldiers coming home was Horace Adams, a fiery redhead who was the son of a store owner in Rome, Georgia. He had married his sweetheart, Glennis, in 1942, just before being drafted and sent to Riverside, California, to begin basic training. Their son, Buford, was born May 28, 1943, around the time Horace

---

3 Words by Frederick W. Faber

departed for Europe, near the end of the European campaign. Horace's job was to enter cities and towns taken by the Allies and rout out any remaining Nazi soldiers. Later, he helped liberate concentration camps and bury the stacked bodies of those they'd been too late to save. After nine months in Europe, he boarded a ship headed to the Pacific. "There wasn't much to eat on that ship," he recalls, "except we had all the Hershey bars we wanted." He ended up in the Philippines and was waiting to invade Japan when the atomic bomb decimated Hiroshima and Nagasaki in August of 1945, forcing Japan's surrender.

The night before he was mustered out of the service, he and his buddies went out drinking to celebrate. Horace says he walked back from the bar, staggering and sick, and thought, *If this is what being drunk feels like, I never want to be drunk again.* At that moment, he decided never to touch alcohol again. And when he got home to Rome, Georgia, his young wife, who had an older brother who had returned from World War Two a hopeless drunk, reinforced that decision by warning that if he ever drank, she would take Buford and leave. She also insisted that they would be in church every time the doors were open.

True to his word, Horace never touched another drop of alcohol. Not even when the farm they were renting failed and he could barely put enough food on the table for their young family. One day, with a little time on his hands, he built a wooden box with compartments for each of their household expenses. Each compartment was labeled in black paint – rent, groceries, heating oil. On Fridays, when he was paid, he would divide the money into those little squares. He added one titled "tithe" because the couple had decided that it was important for them to give ten percent of whatever they earned to God. Everything they had belonged to God, they reasoned. *The Lord gives and the Lord takes away, blessed be the name of the Lord.*

The Lord gave them another son, Gerry. Then He took away the farm. But at the height of their despair over failing as farmers, Horace heard from a relative who owned a grading company in Atlanta. The man needed a bulldozer operator. Atlanta was a good two-hour drive from Rome, so Horace bunked with his relatives during the week and went home on the weekends.

Clayton County is directly south of Atlanta and home to the Atlanta airport. Jonesboro, Georgia, almost twenty miles south of Atlanta, is the seat of Clayton County's government. Its courthouse was destroyed by fire during Sherman's march to the sea at the end of the Civil War, meaning that Clayton County property records prior to the Civil War are virtually untraceable. It is known, though, that a man named Robert Huie purchased nearly one hundred fifty acres in Clayton County around the time of the Civil War, where he lived with his family. William Huie Reynolds, a self-taught lawyer who was most likely a descendent of Robert Huie, purchased the land in the 1920s. One of Horace's first jobs once he got to Atlanta was to build several ponds for William Reynolds, who was by this time a retired Clayton County Superior Court judge.

Horace gradually built up a bit of a rapport with the judge, who could be a bit crotchety. One day, when the project was nearing completion, Judge Reynolds said to him, "I'll bet you're wondering why I'm spending all this money to build these lakes."

Before Horace could respond, Judge Reynolds said, "It ain't none of your damn business. Just build the lakes!"

Horace eventually scraped together enough money to buy a house and move his family to Forest Park, a suburb of Atlanta located in Clayton County. Their older son, Buford, remembers,

"The house cost $6,700. Mom made our bed sheets by sewing four fifty-pound flour sacks together. Our underwear and sheets were made out of flour sacks. And people didn't have dryers back then. You hung your laundry on the clothesline. I still remember being embarrassed as a kid because we were the only people in the neighborhood who had flour sack sheets hanging on our clothesline. We were probably the inspiration for the *Beverly Hillbillies*."

Horace found a better job repairing generators for the Army at Ft. Gillem, the Army Depot in Forest Park. Once the boys started elementary school, Glennis went to work. They managed to purchase the home next door to them and rent it to Horace's sister, Edna, whose husband was an alcoholic. When Edna was at work, Buford and Gerry were sent next door to stay with their younger cousin, Mike. The Adams began to prosper. Every time Horace put money into that wooden bill box, he faithfully set aside ten percent of their earnings for a tithe.

Buford and Gerry remember being in church and Sunday school every week, without fail, at Mount Zion Baptist Church in Morrow, Georgia. Buford tells this story about being a young boy in church: "One Sunday, the preacher was going long. I was bored, and I slipped down and began playing on the floor near my mother's feet. I looked under the pew and thought it would be fun to just roll and see how far I could go. Well, people just kept lifting their feet, and I rolled under the pews all the way to the front of the church. It stopped the preacher when he saw me." Glennis was mortified at having to walk up front and retrieve her son. She marched him home and made him pick out his own hickory switch.

Glennis Adams, my grandmother, died in 2001 after an excruciating battle with pancreatic cancer. Horace is now in his nineties. He still wears his wedding ring and still tears up at the mention of her name.

Grandmom grew up in Texas Valley, just north of Rome, Georgia, during the Great Depression. Her mother died giving birth to her little brother when Grandmom was three years old. After that, she was raised by her older sisters until her father heard about a widow just across the Alabama line. He'd never met the woman, but he wrote her a letter asking her to marry him, and just like that, "Miss Sarah" became their stepmother. She was, by all accounts, very good to Grandmom and her family.

Still, it was a rough childhood. Breakfast was often only a biscuit dunked in a cup of coffee – "soakie" was what they called the concoction. Lunch at school was a hunk of cold cornbread and a cup of buttermilk. But even that didn't last long because she had to quit school after the third grade to help her family pick cotton.

Four months after she died, Granddad called to ask my sister and me if we would come help clean out his attic. He told us that weekend to take anything we wanted. I went away with his old World War Two foot locker, a stack of old family photos, and an antique wash stand. He gave my dad that old wooden box with the compartments for their bills, the one with the category for their tithe.

Children of the Depression and of World War Two never threw anything away. The attic wasn't exactly a potential episode of *Hoarders*, but it was obvious that Grandmom was a bit of a pack rat. That weekend in October 2001, we found piles of old sheets from our own childhood beds in that attic. She'd saved them, I guess, thinking that at some point they could be used as quilting pieces. Old clothes were treated the same way.

We found stacks and stacks of old cards she and Granddad had received over the years. Curiously, those from her generation were signed in pencil. Only those from her children and grandchildren were signed in pen. Grandmom once explained to me that people used to sign cards in pencil so that the signatures could be erased and the cards reused. Alternately, during times when even greeting cards were too much of an extravagance, she and Granddad had driven to the drug store and each of them had picked out a card that said what they wanted to say. But they didn't purchase the cards; they handed them to one another in the drug store, read them, and then went on their way.

Her old cookbooks were hilarious. Next to a recipe she'd tried and liked, she would write: "Good." Just as often, the note next to a recipe would say, "Not good." Or, as she was often quoted as saying aloud, "Not fit to eat." Another thing she saved was jokes. We found tiny slips of paper with jokes jotted down in her handwriting. One went like this: "How do Eskimos have babies? They just rub their noses together and the little boogers fall out."

Obviously, growing up in the circumstances she did never diminished her sense of humor. Grandmom was one of the funniest people I've ever known. In her attic I found a crocheted skunk made to fit over a can of air freshener. Pinned to the skunk was a slip of paper with her handwriting: "For a refreshing odor that never fails, press the button beneath my tail."

I took the photos, wash stand, and foot locker home. One day several months later, I walked past the wash stand, which I'd placed upstairs in the hallway between two of my children's bedrooms, and it occurred to me that I'd never opened its drawers to see what treasures my pack rat of a Grandmother had left in it.

I found an anniversary card Grandmom had given to my grand-father in 1996. Written in it were these words: "We have had 54 great years, and I love you even more than I did then."

That message was written in ink.

Granddad has promised me one more thing from his house after he dies -- a piece of artwork (if you can call it art) that has always caught my attention. It's a simple wooden sign painted with the words "Adams, Est. 1942." For me, it is a perpetual reminder that it's possible to be in love with the same person for an entire lifetime.

And it's important to this story because everything you'll read in the next two hundred and fifty pages began with Horace and Glennis Adams.

God Will Take Care of You

All you may need he will provide
God will take care of you
Nothing you ask will be denied
God will take care of you [4]

Buford was popular at Forest Park High School. He was tall and thin. With his high cheekbones and brown hair that had hints of red when the sun hit it the right way, he was a mixture of both his parents' features (Glennis's Cherokee heritage and Horace's Northern European roots) and their personalities – serious and stable like his dad but with his mother's sense of humor. He was the editor of the school yearbook and a good student. At fourteen, he got a job working for a man named S. Truett Cathy at his restaurant, the Dwarf House, in Forest Park. Buford would walk to the restaurant every day after school and work as a carhop until nine or ten on school nights and until after midnight on weekends. Cathy, who would later invent a chicken sandwich and become the billionaire founder of Chick-Fil-A, saw him as a hard worker and quickly promoted him from busboy to grill

---

4 Words by Civilla Durfee Martin

man, a job he would have into his college years.[5] Buford saved every penny and was able to buy himself a 1950 Ford. He tore four transmissions out of that car by drag racing, and his dad patiently repaired the car every time. But on the fifth time, Horace stood over him and made him do the work. He never ruined another transmission.

A high school friend invited Buford to a meeting called Youth for Christ, an organization that had been led in its infancy by the famed evangelist Billy Graham. It was at one of those meetings Buford committed his life to Christ and began to feel the call to ministry. He became very involved in Youth for Christ and was chosen for leadership positions in the Atlanta chapter. It was at a Youth for Christ meeting one night in 1961 that he met Sandy and Babs Weber, a set of blonde-haired and deeply tanned identical twins who were nearly impossible to tell apart. The twins had recently moved to Atlanta from Miami, Florida, when their father, a pilot, had been transferred there by the airline. Of their first meeting, Buford says, "Babs and Sandy Weber

---

5 In the later years that Buford worked at the Dwarf House, Truett Cathy would occasionally walk into the kitchen carrying a breaded, seasoned chicken breast and ask Buford to fry it for him. "They'd come out kind of hard and crispy on the outside and raw on the inside," Buford says. Cathy kept at it, eventually coming up with the idea to pressure fry the chicken. That was the beginning of the Chick-Fil-A sandwich. In the early days of the sandwich, Cathy sold the breasts, already seasoned and breaded, along with the rights to call them Chick-Fil-A sandwiches, to other restaurants. He eventually grew unhappy with the arrangement because he couldn't control the quality. So he took over the operation and opened the first actual Chick-Fil-A restaurant in 1967 in Greenbriar Mall in Atlanta. It was also the first time that a shopping mall leased out space for a restaurant with a seating area, and that was the beginning of mall food courts.

were the most beautiful girls I had ever seen. I went home that night, and I wrote in my diary, 'I just met the girl I'm going to marry.'"

The twins invited him over to their house one night and played for him an audiotape of a meeting they called "Youth Ranch." Both girls had accepted Christ as their Savior at a Youth Ranch meeting, and they were eager to share it with Buford because they found it to be remarkably similar to Youth for Christ.

The Youth Ranch was started in the late 1950s in Miami by a man named A. Ray Stanford. A decorated World War Two B-17 bomber pilot and former salesman for National Cash Register Company, Stanford was a gifted public speaker and a magnetic personality who had also started Grove Community Church and Florida Bible College. Sandy and Babs had been very involved in the Youth Ranch ministry during their high school years in Miami and eventually persuaded their entire family to become members of the church Stanford pastored.

The twins moved back to Miami after graduating from North Clayton High School, and they enrolled in Florida Bible College. Still determined that he was going to marry one of the Weber twins, Buford felt God's call to also attend Florida Bible College. It was during his time there that he saw a Youth Ranch meeting firsthand and fell in love with the model.

He and Babs were married in August of 1963 and moved to Chattanooga, Tennessee, where Buford continued his studies at Tennessee Temple University. During that time, he led a Bible Study in Etowah, Tennessee, and with a friend named Robert Hughes produced a fifteen-minute public service radio program called Voice of American Youth. A man named Fred Bischoff heard the radio program and contacted Buford. He wanted to know if Buford would be willing to move to St. Petersburg,

Florida, to work for an organization called Truth for Youth.[6] So in June of 1964, the newlyweds moved to St. Petersburg to work for that ministry. Unfortunately, what they were promised and what the organization delivered were two different things. They found out upon their arrival in Florida that they were expected to live at the Truth for Youth building. They put a mattress on the floor and a refrigerator in the corner of one of the offices. Babs recalls the living conditions with a shudder: "At one point our shower was a garden hose strung through the window of the ladies' bathroom." They quickly realized they were miserable and began looking for new work.

In late January 1965, Horace Adams visited his tax preparer, a man named Al Williams, who had a shop on Main Street in Forest Park. Williams noticed receipts for contributions to an organization called Truth for Youth and began asking questions. After Horace explained that his son was a youth minister working for that organization, Williams said, "Well, if Buford and Babs will move to Forest Park and start a ministry, I have six acres with a lake and a swimming pool on it that I'll give them."

That night, Horace sat down and wrote the one and only letter he's ever written to his son. In it, he outlined Williams's offer. Unbeknownst to either of them, Buford penned a letter to his dad the very same night saying he and Babs weren't really happy in St. Petersburg and didn't like what was happening at Truth for Youth. "We feel like the Lord is calling us to move to Atlanta.

---

6 Richard DeHaan also worked for Truth for Youth at the time. On behalf of his father's organization, Radio Bible Class, DeHaan would begin producing the "Day of Discovery" television show in 1968, which is still in production today and is one of the longest-running Christian television shows in the country.

If you happen to hear of any opportunities for youth ministry, please let me know," he told his dad. Those letters crossed in the mail.

Two days later, Babs and Buford drove over the causeway in St. Petersburg to collect the Truth for Youth mail. In it was the letter from Horace. They took that letter as confirmation that God wanted them to move back to Atlanta and gave Bischoff two weeks' notice. They packed what few belongings they had – a sofa, mattress and springs, and a refrigerator – into a U-Haul trailer and headed for Atlanta, Georgia.

Al Williams was giving them the land, but with this caveat: it came with a mortgage that they would have to assume. Williams promised to pay the monthly mortgage by writing a check for $560 to Buford, who would turn around and write a check to the mortgage holder, a man name Joe McCracken.

Their hearts sank at first sight of their new property on Barton Drive in Forest Park. There was no building at all, just an empty swimming pool and a bathhouse next to a small lake, and both of those structures were in sad shape. They moved into a rental house Mr. Williams owned on adjoining property and set about repairing the pool -- painting it and trying to get the plumbing into operating order. Some of the neighborhood kids began to wander by and ask if they could swim. Buford promised a pool party as soon as the pool was fixed.

One of those kids was Jack Bartlett, a thirteen-year-old who spent his summers fishing in the lake on Barton Drive. "In that day, a pool was like Disneyland. Nobody had one. Nobody even had air conditioning, and that was why my friends and I were outside all summer," Jack says. "So when Buford said we could swim, I promised I would be there!"

God Will Take Care of You

The pool was ready in March. The plan was to have a swim party followed by a short meeting. The meeting would be modeled after the Youth for Christ and Youth Ranch ones Buford and Babs had attended as teenagers, meetings that always included music.

Gospel music was a large part of popular culture at the time. In fact, Elvis Presley's version of "Crying in the Chapel" was the current #3 song in the country. So the Gospel songs would be familiar to the teenagers. The only problem was that Buford was no musician, and he had no one to do the music for him. He bought a used guitar for $3 and begged a friend to teach him enough to get by.

In March 1965, Buford and Babs Adams hosted the first meeting of the Atlanta Youth Ranch. Fifteen or twenty neighborhood kids swam in the pool, and then climbed out and sat, dripping wet, on carpet squares that had been scattered around the pool deck for the meeting. Buford sat on an upturned Coca-Cola crate and strummed the three chords he'd learned on that guitar – E, A, and B7. Playing only songs that used those three chords, he encouraged the kids to sing along with him.

Throughout the summer of 1965, they held their meetings under the shelter of the pool house. Someone donated an old soft drink machine to the Youth Ranch, so the attraction for those kids was the free Cokes,[7] swimming, volleyball on a makeshift court, and ping pong on a rickety old table set up next to the pool. The activities were followed by a few Gospel songs and a brief Bible study. Between thirty-five and forty teenagers attended during the first few months, but the crowd grew steadily over the summer.

Buford quickly began making plans to take the teenagers to a youth camp in Boca Raton, Florida, that was hosted by Florida

---

7 or Co-Colas, as they're pronounced in the Deep South

Bible College and Ray Stanford, the man who had been Babs' pastor during her teenage years in Miami. He obtained a list of the football players at Hapeville High School, Forest Park High School, and North Clayton High School, and in the spring of 1966, he sent every one of those boys an invitation to an all-expenses-paid camp in Florida. A couple of days later, Buford got a call from the coaches at Hapeville High School. They were upset, saying, "Our kids got your letter and they're all excited about going to the beach. But you can't take away our players in August. That's when we have football practice."

Buford quickly replied, "Well, why don't you coaches come with us? You can have your football camp down there." And to his surprise, they agreed.

He hung up the telephone, wondering where he would get the money to pay for all those free trips. And how would he transport that many people to Boca Raton, Florida? He called Stanford, who said, "Raise what money you can, and get those kids here. I'll cover what you can't." Buford sent a letter to several supporters explaining the importance of the camp and received several hundred dollars in donations. The Youth Ranch also hosted a fundraising banquet, which would become the first of many, in the upstairs room of Citizen's Bank in Forest Park. The premise of those banquets, of course, was that it was much easier to ask people for money after you had fed and entertained them.

Al Williams, their original benefactor and landlord, bartered with First Baptist Church in Morrow, Georgia, for a decrepit old school bus. Horace Adams got the bus into running shape. Buford remembers, "Every time I filled it up with gas, I'd have to unscrew the gear shift and pull the whole thing out. That left a hole going into the transmission, and I would pour a quart of transmission fluid in that bus because it was leaking so badly," a reminder, perhaps, of all those transmissions he'd ruined as a teenager.

He showed up at Hapeville High School in that beat up old bus on a Saturday night around ten o'clock. Parents looked shocked. They were skeptical about allowing their boys to get on that rattletrap for a long ride to south Florida. The coaches didn't seem too eager to board the bus, either. But they did, and Buford took the entire football team and its coaches to camp. For the first couple of days, he says, they weren't happy about being in a morning Bible study, but as the week went on, they began to enjoy the camp. By the end of the week, they were as excited to be there as Buford was to have them there. More than forty years later, one of those coaches still attends the church.

For the next several years, at the end of the first week of camp, the group left Boca Raton after the last meeting, somewhere around ten o'clock in the evening, driving through the night to Forest Park, arriving around two the next afternoon. Buford would go to bed and take a long nap. Horace would take the bus, clean it up, get it gassed up and ready to go, and about eight o'clock that evening, Buford and the second batch of kids would head to Florida for another week of camp.

It was a long drive, about fourteen hours each way, because the bus couldn't go very fast. But in all those years, there was never a breakdown or even a flat tire. Buford says, "I always stopped in Valdosta, Georgia, at mile marker one at a place called Candyland. It was a strange-looking building that resembled a carousel. I'd call ahead and arrange to have forty cheeseburgers, forty orders of fries, and forty Cokes sitting on the tables ready to be eaten when we walked in." They would arrive between two and three o'clock in the morning, wolf down their burgers, use the restrooms, and be back on the road within fifteen or twenty minutes. No one ever complained, maybe because it was 1966, seven years before Burger King insisted you could "have it your way."

After that first camp, Youth Ranch attendance skyrocketed. Weekly meetings began to average 250 teenagers. Buford stuck to the same simple format for the meetings. Several guys sat on upturned Coke cartons strumming guitars to lead the singing. A washtub fiddle like the one seen on the comedy and variety television show *Hee Haw* added a bit of character to the music. After a few songs, Buford would ask for volunteers to give a testimony. Hands would shoot into the air, and one by one, teens would stand to say, in so many words, that God had changed their lives. Then Buford would sit on a stool in the front of the room and deliver a simple ten-minute message, always ending with an illustration he had learned in Bible college. Called "The Hand Gesture," it went like this:

(Holding up his left hand) "Let this hand represent you and me and this hand (holding up his right hand) represent God." Placing his wallet in his left hand, he would continue, "and let my billfold represent sin. We all have sin on us, and that sin separates us from God, causes a barrier between us. But the Bible says that God loves us and wants us to spend eternity with Him in Heaven, so He sent His only Son, Jesus, to earth to die as a sacrifice for our sin." Taking the wallet out of his right hand and placing it in his left, he said, "Jesus took our sin on Himself so that the barrier separating us and God was removed. And all we have to do is accept that Jesus was our sacrifice, that like the Bible says, 'God made Him who had no sin to be sin for us,' so that we can have a place in Heaven." At that point, he would tell everyone to bow their heads in prayer, asking anyone who wanted to accept Jesus Christ as their Savior to silently repeat this simple prayer:

"God, I know that I have sinned and that Heaven is a perfect place. I can't go there with sin on me. But I also know that you sent your Son, Jesus Christ, to take my sin away, and I accept that free gift. I ask you to be my Lord and Savior. Amen."

Every week, several teenagers would raise their hands to indicate that they had prayed that simple salvation prayer.

By this time, teenagers were crammed into the Adams's rented basement room like sardines. They needed more space, to be sure, but there was another problem: when it rained, the basement flooded. The Youth Ranch needed a building, and they needed it right away.

Around that time, a man named Charles Swift, a fraud investigator for Gulf Oil, was transferred to Atlanta. "Swifty," as he was known to friends and family, was a former City of Miami police officer who had been a friend of Babs and her family during her teenage years in Miami. And part of the Swift family package was Opa, Swifty's father-in-law, who was a retired boat builder.

With Swifty and Opa's help, they started having work parties. A man named Tommy Vaughn, whose daughter was a regular at the Youth Ranch, owned a grading company, and Buford talked him into digging out a basement, basically providing a flat surface on which to site the building. Swifty, Buford, and a handful of teenage boys hand dug the footings one Saturday. Enough contributions came in to be able to pour the footings, and a man named Willie Huddleston, who had graciously consented to serve on the Board of the Youth Ranch, donated the concrete for the foundation from his business, Huddleston Concrete.

Buford remembers the day they poured that floor: "I didn't know how to pour concrete, but we managed to level it enough that it seemed like a decent floor. It always had waves in it, but it worked. We got enough money to buy some cement blocks, and we began laying those blocks ourselves. We did it for two or three straight Saturdays before realizing it was above our capacity." They hired professionals to finish the job. Now they had a foundation and four walls but no money. Construction was at a standstill. At Huddleston's suggestion, they raised $8000 by selling sixteen homemade $500 bonds that would bear 6% interest, with one maturing every six months. And once again, Al Williams came to their rescue. He paid a man named Gus Haynie $4,500 to frame the building and put a roof on it. By doing what they could themselves, they were able to finish the building with the money they had raised. Buford remembers, "We had a lot of help, mostly from Swifty and the kids, but also from parents of some of the kids who would come by on Saturdays and help with odd jobs." What the volunteers couldn't handle was done by Gus Haynie and his crew.

It took about four months to construct the Ranch, which consisted of a giant basement that served as a meeting room and an upstairs apartment for Buford and Babs.

Every six months, one of those bonds would become due, so every six months, they had to come up with $500 plus interest to pay it off.

During the summer of 1966, Joe McCracken, the man who held the mortgage on the property, paid Buford a visit. He angrily stated that Williams was three months behind on the mortgage, and he threatened foreclosure. Desperate, Buford and Babs drove to the Swift's house to ask for advice. Over chocolate nut ice cream sundaes, the two couples discussed how they could raise the money to save the Youth Ranch property. Swifty would later write, "All types of ideas were discussed on how we would get over this hurdle. Our wives felt we should turn it over to the Lord, but they had little experience in the business world and neither knew Mr. McCracken."

The following Saturday, Buford and Swifty were working in the yard when a big car pulled up. Four men in suits got out and introduced themselves as a committee from Delta Airlines sent to evaluate the work of the Atlanta Youth Ranch. They explained that the airline, which had been headquartered in Atlanta since 1941, operated a charitable fund benefitting the city, and a group of Delta employees had nominated the Youth Ranch for a contribution.

The next week, Buford received a check from Delta Airlines that covered the overdue mortgage and late fees with $17 to spare. And for the next several years, the Youth Ranch received $1000 each year in support from that fund.

Joe McCracken's attitude toward the ministry softened after the mortgage was caught up. He became a sympathetic friend of the Ranch, even though most months, Williams's check to the Youth Ranch would bounce, which meant the Youth Ranch's check to McCracken bounced. McCracken would call Buford, and Buford would go to see Williams, who would pull cash out of a drawer for Buford to take to McCracken.

Word spread through Clayton County about the Youth Ranch's success. Most people were happy about the Ranch's ministry to teens, but some were suspicious. For instance, a pastor of a local church called and said to Buford, "I hear y'all are having mixed bathing over at that place."

"No sir. We don't have anyone bathing at our meetings. But we do let kids swim."

Churches in the surrounding area began sending their youth ministers and other representatives to scout out the Youth Ranch meetings. Inevitably, they would arrive with a pen and paper and scribble notes about the upturned Coke crates, the teenagers sitting on carpet squares scattered randomly on the bare concrete floor, the ping pong and volleyball and free Cokes after the meeting. And inevitably, they would go back to their churches, throw carpet remnants on the floor, sing a few songs, give away free Cokes, and then wonder why they couldn't attract the same crowds that the Atlanta Youth Ranch could.

Buford always believed that the difference was very simple. In the first few weeks of the Ranch, he hand picked a few teenagers and put them on what he called his "Council." He taught them to be open and friendly to every single person who showed up to a Thursday meeting, to smile and introduce themselves, and to be genuinely interested in the teenagers who walked through the doors. He encouraged them to read Dale Carnegie's 1936 classic *How to Win Friends and Influence People*. Teenagers will go where they feel comfortable and included, he told his Council, and the Youth Ranch crowds proved his theory to be correct. In addition, a fundraising brochure printed in the early days of the Ranch provides this insight: "The key to the success of the Ranch might be labeled as 'substitutionary involvement.' Instead of being involved in those activities which are detrimental, we keep the young person involved in a purpose: reaching others, just like someone reached him." Many of the teenagers who served on that Council over the years would later go into Christian work. Today, two of them – Jack Bartlett and Toney Jones -- have significant roles in the ministry of Community Bible Church.

Another probable reason the teenagers flocked to the Adams was that Buford and Babs created a great deal of fun. At Halloween that very first year, they staged a haunted trail in the woods around the pool house. They charged admission and used the funds raised to take teenagers to a Christmas camp in the North Georgia mountains.

Using 2x4 boards hung with black plastic, they built a huge maze next to the swimming pool and hung raw meat in it. The teenagers dressed in scary costumes. One boy, Charlie Austin, wanted to be a werewolf, and he persuaded Babs, against her better judgment, to paint his face with rubber cement and put fake hair all over it. Buford remembers, "He looked like a werewolf, but when we tried to take the fake fur off, the rubber cement peeled the top layer of his skin off."

Fun and unfortunate Halloween costumes aside, the Youth Ranch ministry was also successful because Buford and Babs earned the trust of parents. While they connected with teenagers, they also acted as responsible adults under whose supervision teenagers were safe. An incident that occurred in April 1968 demonstrated their determination to act in the best interest of those in their care.

When Martin Luther King, Jr., was assassinated, the entire world watched to see if Atlanta would erupt in race riots. Detroit and Washington, D.C., had, and it was only natural for the city that served as King's home base to be the epicenter of a violent reaction to his murder. National Guard troops were called in to the city, and they surrounded the capitol building in Atlanta, which was only one mile from the place where King preached every week, Ebenezer Baptist Church.

Atlanta Police Chief Herbert T. Jenkins ordered every police officer in the city to be on duty the day of the funeral, the only instance in Atlanta's history in which every member of the force was on duty at the same time. That day, 150,000 people showed up to honor King, and it remains the largest funeral ever held for a private citizen in the United States. To the credit of the City of Atlanta and its Major, Ivan Allen, the personal contributions of Robert Woodruff, who was the head of Coca-Cola and the secret benefactor of many nonprofit organizations, the Atlanta Police force, and the mourners' adherence to Luther's insistence on non-violence, Atlanta was the only major city in the United States that did not have violent demonstrations after the assassination.

But on Monday, April 8, 1968, the day before the funeral, the whole country was holding its breath to see what would happen in Atlanta when King was laid to rest. Buford and Babs were expecting five hundred teenagers from Georgia and Florida for an Easter camp that was to be held at the FHA campground in Covington, Georgia. A group from Pompano, Florida, drove all night, and a boy in that group had slept for several hours on the bus while wearing his hard contact lenses. By the time he got to Covington, the lenses were stuck to his eyeballs, and the kid was in pain. Buford and Babs pulled out a telephone book and called eye doctors all over the city. They finally found a doctor open after hours, but his office was in downtown Atlanta. Babs was terrified, but Buford made the decision to drive into Atlanta, making his way through police barricades by stopping to explain his predicament, and safely delivered the boy to a doctor who could help him.

The Atlanta Youth Ranch enjoyed solid growth and steady financial support for two more years. But it faced a crisis when Al Williams died unexpectedly. All of a sudden, they couldn't afford the mortgage on the property.

God Will Take Care of You

In the late 1960s, foreclosure laws stipulated that if a person foreclosed and wasn't able to recoup the total investment back by re-selling the property, he could go after the mortgagee personally. As Board members, Horace Adams, Buford Adams, and a man named Arnold Yancey were all on the note. In desperation, Buford paid a visit to Pierce Peacock, the president of the Bank of Forest Park. After hearing the story, Peacock grinned and said, "Why, you boys have a gold mine there. You just need to get it zoned for apartments."

"There's no way that could happen," Buford argued. The three-member county commission had recently been accused of taking bribes for zoning inappropriate tracts of land for apartments, and county residents were up in arms over it. The stories were all over the local paper, the *Clayton News/Daily*.

Chuckling, Peacock said, "Y'all go on down to the county commission and make application. Those boys have done enough evil, it's time they did some good."

The night of the zoning hearing, in the summer of 1968, nearly two hundred neighbors showed up in opposition. The commissioners heard the case but refused to make a decision that evening. One of the commissioners, Tommy Vaughn, the same man who had dug out that basement for the building, said, "I've been accused of taking money under the table for apartment zoning, and I'll not vote for another apartment as long as I'm in office." Buford went home that night thinking they would lose the property. But it was the 1960s in the Deep South -- when the commissioners next met to make a decision, the hearing was held in the middle of the day, while the opposition was at work. Zoning was approved for apartments at the Youth Ranch property on Barton Drive in Forest Park.

The property was immediately put on the market. They soon received an offer, one that would pay off the mortgage and give the young ministry approximately $20,000 with which to purchase new property.

While the Youth Ranch was looking for a place to relocate, Buford was facing another hard decision. Many of the parents who had volunteered at the work parties, and some of the Adams' close friends, were urging him to start a church. They wanted to hear the same messages he was giving to the teenagers. But Buford had been resisting for two reasons. First, he had always felt called to youth ministry. He liked working with teenagers because, as he put it, teens are making the most important decisions of their lives – who they would spend their life with and what they would spend their life doing. Adults, he felt, were already set in their ways and not as pliant. Secondly, he and Babs were members of Colonial Hills Baptist Church in East Point. They adored their pastor, Paul VanGorder, and felt that it would be a slap in his face if they went out and started a new church.

Buford told his potential congregation that he needed to pray about the decision. He did, and within a few months, he received a sign he felt was directly from God. VanGorder retired from his position as pastor after suffering a heart attack. Not long after his departure, a young African-American man named Tony Evans, a professor at Carver Bible College in Atlanta, tried to join the church congregation. It was the late 1960s, and Atlanta was rife with racial tension. The church held a congregational meeting on a Tuesday night, and Buford recalls the new pastor, VanGorder's successor, standing before the crowd and saying, "Our board has decided we will not accept black members in our church or black children in our school. That's our stand, and we're not changing. If you disagree, we'll still be friends, but we ask you to part with us and let us have our decision stand." The Adams were appalled. The God they served didn't exclude anyone. But that sealed Buford's decision. After asking for and receiving VanGorder's blessing, he agreed to serve as pastor for the nascent membership until someone more suitable for the job could be found.

Interestingly, Tony Evans went on to become the first African-American to earn a doctoral degree from Dallas Theological Seminary. He has served as chaplain for the Dallas Mavericks and the Dallas Cowboys, and is the pastor of the 9,000-member Oak Cliff Bible Fellowship in Dallas, Texas. He is the author of over fifty books, and his daily radio broadcast, *The Alternative with Dr. Tony Evans*, can be heard on more than five hundred radio stations in over forty countries. Paul VanGorder began writing regularly for *Our Daily Bread* and became a speaker on the *Day of Discovery* television program after leaving Colonial Hills. He died in 2009.

Colonial Hills Baptist Church is no longer in Atlanta. It moved thirty miles west of the city in the mid-1990s, and an African-American congregation now owns the East Point property.

Clayton Community Church held its first services in late 1969 in the Youth Ranch meeting room with about thirty-five people in attendance. The Adams' living room housed the nursery. Becky Russell, one of the Youth Ranch teenagers, plunked out hymns on an out-of-tune piano that was missing several keys, and people shared the few hymnals they'd managed to procure before Buford stood to deliver a sermon.

An engineer from south Florida named Bob Kohl, one of the church's founding members, hand wrote the church's statement of faith and governing documents. Without any formal legal training, he figured out how to incorporate the infant church, which would continue "searching" for a permanent pastor for thirty-four years.

I was born in February 1967, not quite two years after the Youth Ranch's first meeting. I'm no expert on memory, but one theory on the subject that interests me is the idea that we are able to repress traumatic events. I suppose I should say that the converse of that theory is what interests me because I hope it means that those who remember a great deal about their childhood and who do not have huge memory gaps were happy growing up. That's how I feel about being raised in this ministry.

My earliest childhood memory had to have happened when I was barely two. My little brother, Beau, was born in February 1969, and in the months before his birth, I'm told, I introduced everyone I met to my imaginary friend, a fuzzy blue-gray guy named Friend Bear. Alas, Friend Bear went away forever when Beau was born. But my very first memory is this: I'm standing on the concrete slab outside of the Ranch meeting room talking to a group of teenagers. A pickup basketball game is going on behind them. They're asking me about Friend Bear. Where is Friend Bear, they want to know. I think for a moment and then, pointing to the pickup game, say, "He's inside that basketball."

The teenagers start laughing, and I remember the delicious feeling of making someone laugh. I'm not sure it's possible for a kid to feel more adored than I did growing up around those teenagers.

I remember the first church "nursery" in the living room of our house, how we could hear the grownups singing downstairs.

My cousins, mom's twin sister Sandy's kids, were there with Beau and me, along with the Kohl's daughter, Dottie.

I remember seeing apartments being built behind our house and hearing my parents talk about moving. I remember the new apartment and my room in it. There was a balcony over the Ranch and church meeting room, and we denizens of the nursery watched the meetings from there. Opa built us a tree house, and when it was finished, Beau told him he'd put it in the wrong tree.

I remember my little sister, Holly, being born. I was five, so I didn't quite understand that she was born prematurely because of Rh factor. I just knew she was sick and couldn't come home from the hospital. I remember Swifty and Arnette driving us to the hospital to drop my mom off so that she could feed Holly. Someone in the car pointed to the big, bright moon and said that there really was a man on the moon.

Over forty years later, as I recall these childhood memories, I'm compelled to check my memory against history. Holly was born on December 14, 1972. Apollo 17, the last manned Apollo mission, landed on the moon December 7 and returned to Earth on December 19. There truly was a man on the moon that night.

But my memories are getting ahead of the story.

How Firm a Foundation

How firm a foundation, ye saints of the Lord
Is laid for your faith in His excellent word[8]

A local realtor named Rudolph Johnson[9] found ten acres for sale on Reynolds Road in Morrow, about ten minutes away from the Ranch's Barton Drive location. Interestingly, the property was across the street from the ponds Buford's father, Horace, had built for Judge William Reynolds nearly twenty-five years earlier. The property was cheap, only $10,000, because five of the ten acres were under a power line easement and almost four were in a swamp. Still, it seemed to have just enough space on which to put a building, although the creek on the property meandered through the only buildable spot, and the only access to Reynolds Road was through a flood plain. Bill Barton, one of the Youth Ranch's original benefactors, brought over a tractor and took down part of a hill under the power easement, using that dirt to make a driveway to access the building site from Reynolds Road.

---

8 Published in John Rippon's *Selection of Hymns*, 1787

9 Johnson, who lived with his family on Reynolds Road north of the church, would become a longtime, faithful member of the church. He would also go on to serve in the Georgia State Legislature from 1971 to 1988.

Judge Reynolds, who was retired by this time, showed up when they began moving the dirt around and said to Buford, "Y'all ought not be building in a swamp."

Buford acknowledged that he was probably right, then said, "But we don't have a choice. This is the only property we could afford."

Then the Youth Ranch hired someone to come in with a dredging machine to straighten out the creek and move it back a couple of feet so that it ran right along the property line, giving them more usable land.[10] A furious Judge Reynolds returned, this time demanding to know who gave them the authority to block his creek. Being upstream from the church, he was afraid altering it would cause the creek to overflow its banks on his property. Buford calmed the old judge down by explaining that they weren't trying to harm his property in any way and showing him exactly what they had done to the creek.[11] But after that, the judge stopped by on a regular basis to make sure they hadn't dammed up the creek.

Buford says that the judge started out almost as an opponent to the church and its ministry. He thought of them as the crazy bunch down in the swamp. "Truthfully, Judge Reynolds was angry that we were even there at all," Buford remembers, adding that over time, friendly gestures toward the old man softened him up so that he eventually became a good friend to the ministry. Over the years, Buford made regular visits to Judge Reynolds just to make sure he was happy. During those visits, he talked to him about Christianity. The judge would usually just chuckle

---

10 Of course, this would be forbidden today. In 1970, it was not illegal.
11 If the creek did overflow, the water filled the floodplain behind the church property owned by Georgia Power that was used as a power line easement.

and say he wasn't interested. But one day he looked at Buford and said, "You know, I really wish I could believe what you believe."

The Youth Ranch and church sold more bonds, raised another $10,000, and procured enough donated materials and labor to begin construction. The new building's plans included a meeting room with a second-level balcony overlooking it, an office, and an apartment for the Adams.[12] Just like with the very first building, Buford hired Gus Haynie in a handshake agreement to be the general contractor for the new Ranch. Their arrangement, once again, was that Haynie would take care of anything they couldn't do on their own or with donated labor and that he would do it at an appropriate price. Buford says, "I still remember Jack Bartlett and I climbing two stories high and catching roof trusses as the crane brought them in. We were scared to death, but we managed to set them into place."

Gus Haynie was a good ol' Southern boy with a pot belly and construction boots that were perpetually unlaced. He was right-handed, but he played golf left-handed so that his brother-in-law wouldn't borrow his clubs. His filing system was to throw things onto the dashboard of his old pickup truck. He had three employees -- Mr. Hand, an ancient fellow who drove an old Ford with no back window, a guy named James, and Asa, an old African-American gentleman who cleaned up the projects. Asa liked to say that his contract ended at the first step of a ladder, meaning he refused to climb anything. Haynie and his crew always got the job done, but because they were depending upon a great deal of donated materials and labor, the process was slow. To complicate the situation, the developer who had purchased the Barton Drive property had promised to let them continue meeting at Barton Drive while the new building was under construction, but not

---

12 By this time, their second child, Beau, had joined the family.

long after construction began, he changed his mind and started building the new apartments. He tore up the volleyball court and left the parking lot a sea of mud. Finishing the Reynolds Road building became urgent.

In October 1969, the Youth Ranch held its first meeting in the new building. Teenagers sat on a bare concrete floor because carpet hadn't yet been installed. In fact, the musicians played their guitars while sitting on a large roll of carpet that was waiting to be laid. There were no tiles in the drop ceiling yet, and the lights were bare bulbs. Rather than it being a melancholy event, Jack Bartlett remembers the first meeting in the new building as exciting. They'd moved on to something bigger and better.

Thankfully, by the next Sunday morning, Buford had procured enough folding metal chairs for the church congregation to have proper seating at its first service on Reynolds Road. The morning after that service, the phone in Buford's office rang. The caller identified himself as the pastor of New Testament Baptist Church, a small congregation that met in a windowless brick building just north of the church's new location. "What were y'all doing down there yesterday?" the man asked.

"We were having church," Buford said.

"I thought y'all was a youth ministry."

"We are, but we're also a church."

The man grunted and said, "There ain't room for two churches on Reynolds Road."

Once the church had settled into the new building and managed to pave a small parking lot, the congregation began to grow. Within a year, attendance averaged one hundred people, which meant that with chairs, they already filled up the brand new Youth Ranch meeting room. Cribs were rolled into the office on Sunday mornings for the nursery, and the Adams's apartment became the Sunday school room for older children. Buford quickly realized that the church would not grow larger than space permitted, so he began thinking about constructing a building solely for the new church. There was still a lot of dirt under the power line easement, and he wondered if it could be used to fill in the swamp. (It was early 1971, and the EPA, which had been formed in December 1970, wasn't yet protecting wetlands).

Buford called the chairman of the Clayton County Board of Commissioners, a man named Charley Griswell, and said, "Charley, we really need a pad for a volleyball court, and we need a larger parking lot. I wonder, since we're a non-profit youth ministry, and we have a couple hundred teenagers coming to these meetings every Thursday night, would you consider bringing some county equipment over to take dirt from the power line easement and fill in the swamp?"

Griswell said, "I think I can do that." The next Monday morning, four large earth moving machines were at 5900 Reynolds Road, and they started pulling dirt from under those power lines and filling in the swamp. When he saw the machines in the parking lot, Buford quickly called Gus Haynie, who agreed to meet him for breakfast. They sat down, and Buford said, "We need to figure out where to put a church building on that property and get that building going."

"How big do you want the building?" Haynie asked.

"Fifty feet wide and a hundred feet long, two stories, with an auditorium upstairs and Sunday school space downstairs," was Buford's quick reply. Haynie pulled out a pen, and the two drew up a plan sitting at that breakfast table in Anne's Fine Foods on Highway 54 in Morrow. Then they drove back to the property and staked out a place for that building. Haynie stopped one of the operators and asked him to dump three feet of extra dirt in the place they had staked out. By that afternoon, the church had a prepared site for what would become its first building.

Clayton Community Church immediately started another fundraising campaign. They issued more bonds, and after a few months, Buford was able to call Gus Haynie and initiate another handshake agreement for a building. Just like the ones before it, this "contract" stipulated that the church would do what they could and Haynie would finish what they couldn't do. Because the building was to be set on what was essentially reclaimed wetland, the foundation needed to be shored up. Construction began with eighteen telephone poles being pounded several feet into the ground and then sawed off to act as piers for the concrete foundation. Over the years, heavy rainstorms caused some concern, yet the building never flooded. That 20,000-square foot building, which still stands solid as a rock over forty years later, was built in a swamp with donated labor for less than $8 per square foot.

It was 1973. The Vietnam War had just ended, and the Watergate scandal was beginning to heat up. To honor the completion of that new building, the church organized a gigantic Easter celebration for April 22. Buford says, "It occurred to us that one way to get attention would be to have a giant Easter egg hunt and maybe fly in the Easter bunny in a helicopter. To my knowledge, this had never been done before."

The Youth Ranch and church owned a printing press. A few years before, a man named George Pace, who did all the printing for Carver Bible College in Atlanta, found an old used press that was very cheap because it needed a great deal of work. Together, he and Buford refurbished it, replacing the old rollers and getting it into good working condition. All printed materials for the entire ministry would come off of that press well into the 1970s.

In preparation for that Easter service in 1973, the church created what looked like a handwritten letter from the Easter bunny and mailed a copy to every home in Clayton County. It was an invitation for children to come see the bunny land in a helicopter and then participate in a massive Easter egg hunt. In the days leading up to Easter Sunday, volunteers were frantically trying to get the new building finished in time for the services. Buford remembers, "We built the choir loft and platform, had the church carpeted, and hung all the light fixtures, put all the chairs together in rows and fastened them together. It was a huge work party on Saturday, the day before, to get ready, but that Easter Sunday was an incredibly successful day." Twelve hundred people attended the morning service, and out of that crowd, many became regular members of the church. Some are still members to this day.

The fledgling church was roundly criticized by older, more established ones in the area for secularizing a religious holiday. It was not the first time the ministry had incurred the wrath of other congregations, and it certainly would not be the last. Interestingly, Easter Sunday egg hunts at church are more the rule than the exception today.

The new space allowed the church to grow rapidly. Buford was baptizing new members nearly every week. He laughs, remembering one of those early baptism services:

"We had just completed construction of our first church building. Being a community church with beliefs somewhere between Baptist and Presbyterian, we had to make a decision on how we would baptize people. We elected to baptize by immersion. That meant putting a person completely under water instead of sprinkling a little on the top of the head. Of course, if you're gonna dunk someone, you've got to have a tank of water to do it, and until the completion of our building, we had no way of baptizing anyone.

"So it was a day of great anticipation and excitement. We had a long list of people waiting to be immersed. They were decked out in the latest baptism fashions purchased from the Southern Baptist bookstore -- blue plastic culottes, which were approved by all congregations because you couldn't see through them when they got wet.

"I pulled my bass fishing waders on over my Sunday morning suit and clipped on a small microphone that was attached to a very long cord, praying I wouldn't get electrocuted when I entered the water. The water was up to my chest. I stood in front of several hundred parishioners. It was a solemn, holy moment.

"The baptistry was a pre-fab plastic tank much like the pre-fab shower stalls you see in mid-range homes. It was, of course, slick when wet. And since we'd tried to save every possible expense in constructing that church building, we'd neglected to put non-slip treads on the steps.

"First up was a guy named Bob. He was about six-six and all of 150 pounds. His culottes only came to about mid-thigh. His legs looked like two hairy ropes with knots tied in them for knees. I intoned a few words about the solemnity of the occasion and then motioned for Bob to join me in the water.

"His foot hit that first step, and both legs shot straight out. All the congregation saw was two hairy legs and blue plastic flying through the air.

"All I could see was about five hundred people laughing themselves silly. I had no idea how to regain control, so I chose to just help Bob secure his footing. My waders had filled with water, so it took two people to pull me out of the baptistry, and I had to preach in a wet suit. I lost a microphone and ruined a suit that day, but I learned something. After that, I always held baptisms at the end of the service."

Buford soon realized he couldn't do a proper job of leading both the church and the youth ministry, so in 1973, he began looking for someone to take the Youth Ranch. Toney Jones had shown up at one of the very first Ranch meetings as a teenager, and he had been a regular ever since. He had been very popular in high school and had gone on to graduate from Bible college. "I always wondered if he was the inspiration for the Fonz," Buford says, because wherever Toney went, a group of teenagers followed. He seemed to be a natural choice to run the youth ministry, so Buford handed the reins of the Youth Ranch to Toney and began to focus solely on the church.

Buford made it a point to personally call on every family that visited the church. Every Tuesday night, Wednesday night, and Saturday morning, he drove all over Clayton County and even some surrounding counties to knock on the doors of those church visitors and personally thank them for attending the church. "Today, pastors don't do that. In the first place, today's church visitors don't want you disturbing their evening, and then there's the safety issue," Buford says. He remembers one particular Tuesday evening visit. "I put my suit on because in those days preachers were expected to wear dark suits. And I had a new pair of dress shoes Babs had bought for me that day. They were nice black leather and more than we could really afford on my preacher's salary. I kissed Babs goodbye and took off." The first address was in the next county to the south, a good twenty-five miles away. His map took him down a dirt road that had been newly cut through the Georgia red clay. The road was barely passable because it had rained for two days straight.

"Finally, through the drizzling rain and darkness, I found the right mailbox. The home sat high on a hill three or four hundred feet off the road, and like the road, the driveway was solid mud. There was no way my two-wheel drive sedan could climb that hill.

"I almost turned around and left, but duty called. I climbed out of the car and started walking up the muddy driveway toward the house. My new shoes were covered in red clay by the time I stepped onto the porch and rang the bell.

"The husband opened the door and acted surprised to see me. Think about it. What nut case would drive twenty-five miles, go down an impassable road on a rain-soaked night, walk up a muddy driveway in a suit and dress shoes to say, 'Thanks for coming to church'? You would have thought I didn't know telephones existed."

Buford politely took off his shoes before entering the home. They had a nice visit, and he was pleased to note that the couple seemed to have really enjoyed church. They even indicated they planned to return the next Sunday. His work done, Buford thanked them for their time and hospitality and said goodnight.

Only one of his shoes was waiting for him on the front porch. The husband said, "Oh, no, that damn dog!" and went running through the rain to a small barn. He returned and sheepishly held the shoe out to Buford, saying, "He chewed on it just a little bit."

"A little bit? That dog had eaten off the entire back of the shoe. It looked more like a bedroom slipper than a shoe," Buford laughs now at the memory. "The man just laughed nervously and said, 'I'm sorry. He just likes to chew on shoes. We'll try to be there Sunday.'"

The couple never showed their faces at church again.

I Am Loved at Community Bible Church

We moved out of the Youth Ranch building apartment and into a rental house about a half-mile from the church before I started first grade. There were two reasons for that move. First, the church needed the space occupied by our little apartment. Second, and more importantly, my mom realized one day that she wasn't cut out for parsonage life. On that day, she was in her bedroom breastfeeding my sister when two men walked into the room. They were Youth Ranch contributors taking a tour. Mom was incensed that they hadn't bothered to knock, and she insisted that day that our family move to a private house.

During those early days of the church, my grandparents, Horace and Glennis Adams, often took us out to lunch after church at the Shoney's Big Boy in Forest Park. I couldn't have been more than six or seven years old, but I can still taste the Shoney's Hot Fudge cake my grandparents always let me order. And I remember thinking as I sat at the table with my parents, my siblings, my grandparents, my aunt and uncle, Donna and Gerry Adams, and my cousins, how lucky I was that my grandparents went to the same church that I did.

Praise Him, All Ye Little Children

Praise Him, praise Him, ye little children,
God is love, God is love[13]

Judge Alvin Foster was a former Georgia state senator who became a State Court Judge in Clayton County in the late 1960s. As a close friend of Herman Talmadge, who was a Senator from Georgia and the son of Eugene Talmadge, Georgia's Governor during the 1930s and 40s, Foster was politically well connected. In 1973, he brought a check for $1000 to Buford and said, "I want you to use this to start a Christian School."

Buford remembers Foster as generous, good to the church, and a devoted church member. "I realize that $1000 wasn't much when you were starting a school," he says, "but we already had the classroom space in the basement of the church building. I called a friend of mine and asked if he'd be interested in being the principal of a Christian School."

Robert Rohm had been one of the Youth Ranch teenagers, and he was married to Donna Lopez, one of the original Youth Ranch kids. Robert had gone on to finish Bible college and was working as a youth pastor in Atlanta. He accepted the offer, and Clayton

---

13 Author anonymous

Christian School opened its doors in September 1973 with thirty-five students in kindergarten and first grade. By 1979, enrollment would top five hundred.

Between 1969 and 1971, labor leaders, women's organizations, and early childhood advocates lobbied Congress for a universal childcare policy. President Nixon vetoed the Comprehensive Child Development Act of 1971, but it brought national attention to the fact that with more women joining the workforce, demand for childcare was only going to increase. Churches already had nurseries and childcare facilities in place for Sunday mornings, space that stood empty on weekdays, so it was a natural progression for them to begin offering daycare services during the week. Their nonprofit status meant they could provide more reasonable rates than for-profit centers, and for the most part, people trusted religious institutions to care for their children. Buford's mother, Glennis, was the daycare director for a nearby church, Conley First Baptist, but in 1973, the church recruited her to start their daycare and preschool program.

Having quit school to help on the family farm during the Depression, she had a third grade education. But from 1973 to her retirement in 1976, Glennis taught scores of four-year-old pre-schoolers their ABCs, phonics, and how to count. She believed in the power of rhyme, so she taught everything with a song or a poem. And she was famous for this phrase: "God gave us two ears and only one mouth so we can listen more than we speak!"

It quickly became apparent that the school was going to be a success. During that first year of its existence, the church borrowed $80,000 from Clayton State Bank to bump out the back end of the Ranch building about one hundred feet, giving them room for six to eight classrooms on each floor. Once again, Buford called Gus Haynie. After explaining to Haynie that he needed the building's extension to be twenty feet wider than the existing building, Buford asked how that was going to look. "Like tits on a boar hog" was Haynie's answer, but he took the job. In addition, what had been the Adams's apartment was converted into church offices on the upper floor and a large commercial kitchen for preparing school lunches on the first floor. The new classroom space was ready for the start of the school year in the fall of 1974.

Not long after the school opened, Buford was sitting in his office one day when a big, burly man burst through the door flashing a badge and demanding to know who had opened a school without the proper permits. "I guess that would be me," Buford answered before asking the man what he needed.

"I'm the state Fire Marshall, and, and you can't just go putting kids in a building that doesn't meet proper fire code," the man belted out.[14]

"I didn't know anything about fire codes and permits for schools," Buford says, shrugging apologetically as he tells the story. "We'd just decided to open a school and hadn't thought anything was different for a school than for a church." He apologized to the Fire Marshall and tried to calm him down by promising the school would do what it took to be within code. The Fire Marshall settled down and handed Buford a list of violations: for starters, the building had no exit signs and exit doors had just doorknobs where panic apparatus should have been. The sheetrock was too thin (fire could spread too quickly), and fire extinguishers needed to be available and visible.

---

14 Buford isn't exactly sure of the date on this, but in Elder's meeting minutes from 1975, there are a couple of references to State Rep. Rudolph Johnson, who was a church member, interceding with the Fire Marshall on the church's behalf.

Fortunately, the Fire Marshall didn't shut the school down. But he did give Buford a deadline for getting the buildings within code. "It cost us a bunnnnch of money," Buford says, and it also put the church and school on the Fire Marshall's "watch list" for many years to come.

It's no secret that many of the church schools started in the late sixties and early seventies were opened as a way of skirting the desegregation of schools mandated by the Civil Rights Act of 1964. During August of 1975, Colonial Hills Christian School in East Point, the school affiliated with the church that rejected Tony Evans as a member in the late sixties, refused to accept an African-American student who applied for admission. The school was ordered by the government to accept the student or face the possibility of losing their tax-exempt status and most likely being forced to pay back taxes. The school was closed for a week while school officials made a decision, and they ultimately chose to accept the student.

At the time, Clayton Christian School did not have its own school board. All decisions regarding the school were made by the church's Board of Elders. On September 7, 1975, the Elders discussed the situation at Colonial Hills, and then a motion was made to accept students at Clayton Christian regardless of race. The motion was passed unanimously, although the decision might not have been so much about race as it was economics. As Buford puts it, "We were anxious to have every kid in our school because more students meant more tuition."

In January 1979, the *Henry and Clayton Sun* newspaper did an extensive article on the school. The reporter who interviewed Robert Rohm asked him about the perception that Christian schools were nothing more than "segregation academies." Robert responded, "All they have to do is come out here and look. We're well integrated. We have children from several different minorities. You might say, 'Well that's only a few.' But we have [accepted] all that's applied."

In a June 1975 Elders' meeting, the Board decided to dispose of the school's charter and place it under the church's to secure its non-profit status. Little did anyone in that room on that summer night know that the school being part of the church's charter would become significant many years later.

Robert was a principal who thought big, and he was also always in search of a bargain. His father, Morris Rohm, was a wealthy businessman in Griffin, Georgia, who heard that the new church needed folding chairs. He and Robert took Buford to a dusty little store in downtown Atlanta. Morris Rohm, a little man with a penchant for large cigars, raked his finger through the dust on a folding chair and said to the proprietor, "Abe, looks like this chair has been here a long time. How much you want for it?"

"Five dollars."

"What if I buy five hundred?" Morris Rohm asked.

"I'll sell them to you for $3.33 apiece."

Morris Rohm quickly said, "Fine. I'll take fifty."

Buford was impressed enough with the senior Rohm's negotiating skills that he sent Robert in search of enough desks to outfit the new classrooms – one hundred would have been sufficient. Robert came back with the exciting news that he'd gotten such a good discount that he'd purchased five hundred desks. "We had nowhere to store them," Buford remembers, shaking his head. Eventually, the school would need that many desks. But for the remainder of Rohm's tenure at the school, Buford insisted on approving all purchases before Robert made them.

I Am Loved at Community Bible Church

Sandee Sumrall taught first grade during the school's inaugural year. I was in that class. Our room was on the ground floor of the new church building. We had chapel with Mr. Rohm in the upstairs auditorium one day a week, and he promised us that very first year that he would give a new Bible to every kid who memorized the books of the Bible. I still have my copy, with the inscription "To Sandi Adams, from Rev. Robert Rohm, May 30, 1974." And to this day, I can rattle off the books of the Bible.

Mr. Rohm also ran children's church, which was called "Super Church" in those days. He was an epic storyteller who brought the stories of the Old Testament to life. I can see him in the front of the room acting out Joseph and his coat of many colors, David and Goliath, and Daniel in the lions' den. And this: he once swallowed a live goldfish in front of Super Church. I can't recall the circumstances; he probably promised to do it if we reached a certain number of kids in attendance. But I have a vivid mental picture of him holding that little orange fish by the tail, raising his arm in the air, tilting his head back, opening his mouth wide, and dropping that poor little guy into his mouth.

The *Henry and Clayton Sun* newspaper article (dated January 18, 1979) made me laugh. In it, Robert uses multiplication tables as an example of something teachers had to force students to memorize. He goes on to say that a teacher's role is to tell students, "You're going to learn this math or I have 3,000 ways to make you miserable." It's funny because along with the books of the Bible, I can also still rattle off all of the multiplication tables. That was, of course, in the days before Common Core.

Victory in Jesus

And then I cried, "Dear Jesus,
Come and heal my broken spirit,"
And somehow Jesus came and bro't
To me the victory [15]

The Independent Baptist church was the fastest growing denomination in the United States in the 1970s. Buford, being fairly new to the job of pastoring a church and open to try anything that would help it grow, began to model the fastest growing churches in America in hopes of having the same success at Clayton Community.

Jack Hyles was one of the leading figures in the Independent Baptist movement. The pastor of First Baptist Church of Hammond in Hammond, Indiana, Hyles is probably most noted for increasing his church attendance by busing in thousands of people. In 1975, *Time* magazine described his bus ministry in an article titled, "Superchurch," which noted that a record church attendance of 30,560 people (up from the normal 14,000) on March 16, 1975, was due to a contest between two bus route teams. That year, the First Baptist of Hammond bus route ministry consisted of 1,000 workers using 230 buses to ferry as many as 10,000 people to church every Sunday.

Buford and Jack Bartlett drove to Hammond, Indiana, to see Hyles's church. Inspired by that bus ministry, they returned to Clayton County and started one of their own. They found six used buses for sale by a school district near Washington, D. C., and purchased them for about $1000 each. After repainting them, the church started six bus routes, mostly through apartment complexes. The bus captain and some volunteers for each route would knock on every door on the route and invite people to ride their bus to the Sunday morning service. At the height of the church's bus minis-try, an average of two to three hundred children and a handful of adults rode one of ten buses to church. Buford says, "We were one of several churches doing the same thing, and after two or three years of this, I began to realize that several buses from compet-ing churches were going through the same apartment complexes, and depending on what each church was offering that particular Sunday – primarily free food or prizes for the kids – they'd pick that bus." Realizing they weren't truly reaching the unchurched but rather merely competing against other churches for numbers, Buford decided that the bus ministry should be phased out.

He also began to see the flaws in the Independent Baptist movement and to pull away from that influence. Fundamentalists to the very core, the Independent Baptists were serious about the beliefs shared by most Christian denominations -- primarily, that Jesus is the only way to God and that salvation is through faith in Christ. But in addition to those basic doctrinal beliefs, they also had very strict rules of conduct. For instance, a common belief of that denomination is that women should not wear pants. Based on verses in the New Testament stating that women should "adorn themselves in modest apparel" (I Timothy 2:9 and I Peter 3:3), the belief is that pants are man's apparel and, therefore, dresses of appropriate length are the preferred "modest" choice for women.

"We were probably more fundamental in those early years than we are today. In fact, there's no doubt about it. We were almost legalistic. Not quite as bad as the Independent Baptists, but we flirted with that," Buford admits.

Oddly enough, it would be the Christian School that provided the impetus for fully backing away from the Independent Baptist influence. The ban on "men's clothing" presented a problem for girls' athletics. Shorts of any kind were, of course, prohibited, and some schools went so far as to ban girls' sports altogether. The others bent a bit and approved culottes for women's athletic wear. For a while, the rules were simply a nuisance; mothers who wore pants to see their sons or daughters play away games were turned away at some gyms.[16] Then the more legalistic schools began demanding that they be able to set the dress code for other schools' facilities. "That's where I drew the line," Buford says.

Dad may have drawn the line against fundamentalism at 5900 Reynolds Road, but it was a ninety-pound Clayton Christian School girl who set some Independent Baptists straight on their home court. During my sixth grade year, our Christian

---

16 In February 1982, the boys' varsity basketball team made it to region championships. A woman named Claire Redman drove to Mt. Vernon Baptist Church in Stockbridge to watch her son David play but was turned away at the door because she was wearing pants. She walked back out to her car, got in, shut the door, and rolled her pant legs up so that they weren't visible beneath her long trench coat. Then she walked back to the gym, paid her admission fee, and watched her son play.

school was scheduled to play an away volleyball match at another Christian school in Atlanta, one that was affiliated with an extremely fundamentalist church. We were wearing long shorts that went all the way to our knees, but when we showed up to play, the other school refused to approve our apparel on the grounds that it was immodest. Our knees were showing. The solution they offered was that we play in long black culottes -- basically long, flared, split skirts -- that they provided. It was an exceptionally clever power play because the one-size-fits-all polyester pants were big enough that we could fit a girl in each leg. They literally slid down our hips. We would have had to forfeit the match had our host school not been kind enough to provide a box of safety pins.

We walked onto the volleyball court wearing pants pinned at the waist and pinned to our shirts to keep them from falling off. Cynthia, a skinny girl who was a pit bull in a Chihuahua body, was so enraged that she hung back in the locker room after the rest of us went onto the court. She took the four or five remaining pairs of culottes and stuffed them down the toilet, flushed, then marched out of the gym and went to the team bus to wait for the match to be over.

The bus ride home was quiet at first. We all wondered if Cynthia would be suspended from school. Would she be kicked out? Or kicked off our volleyball team? We all sympathized with her and probably all wished we'd done the same thing.

It was our practice, in those early days of the school, whether we'd won or lost, to sing the old Gospel song "Victory in Jesus" on the bus ride home. Maybe it was my imagination, but everyone seemed to sing just a bit louder that day.

I told my parents what happened when I got home, and my dad rolled with laughter. I think he was amused by the fact it took a skinny eighth grader to finally stand up to the fundamentalists.

Victory in Jesus

I was happy when Mr. Rohm told Cynthia that he didn't condone what she'd done but only made her write a letter of apology to the other school. We never played that school again.

Maybe it's just my perception, but that event seemed to be the climax of the fundamentalist bent at the church and school. After that, we became the school that didn't try to dictate every aspect of a student's life. The practical result was that the school experienced incredible growth. But it was also around that time that the fundamentalists began referring to us as Satan Community Church and Christian School.

In the Garden

And He walks with me, and He talks with me,
And He tells me I am His own;
And the joy we share as we tarry there,
None other has ever known.[17]

Being the pastor of a church, of course, meant preparing sermons. Buford had honed his public speaking skills with the radio show and the short Youth Ranch messages. But a forty-five-minute sermon required much more preparation.

He describes his process: "I was doing one of two things in a sermon -- either preaching through a book of the Bible so that I had a mandated text that I had to preach from (the next ten verses or chapter, etc.), or I was doing a topical sermon, usually one in a series. If I was preaching through a text, I would scour that text for the central idea. If I was doing a topical sermon, I would summarize what I wanted to say in one simple declarative sentence. Either way, it was about the same process: the basic idea in building a sermon is to be able to articulate the main idea of that sermon in one simple sentence.

"If you're preaching an expository message (that is, a verse-by-verse message explaining Scripture) then your points in the sermon should come from those verses. If you're preaching a

---

17 Written by C. Austin Miles

topical sermon, then you can skip around in Scripture and build your points on any verse that supports your central idea. Once you have your basic premise of the sermon -- your thesis -- then you build your points. Each point must support that thesis. And after each point in the sermon, you need to have an illustration or a joke to lighten it up. You make the point and that's a serious point, and then you need to lighten it with either humor or an anecdote. Then, in conclusion, you restate the central idea of the sermon, and it's good to end with something like a joke or a true story that leaves people feeling good about having been in church. Of course, you have to be very careful about time. It's very easy, especially after you've been preaching for a while, to get long-winded. So you need to rehearse your sermon. I used to go through it in my mind five or six times before I got up there on Sunday morning so that I could time it and make sure I wouldn't speak too long."

That is the long version of how he built sermons. The short version? He often quipped that a good sermon basically contained "three points and a poem."

Once particular Sunday, when Buford was waxing eloquent on the subject of Satan's sinister influence, a well-dressed middle-aged woman stood up and said in a loud voice, "I have a message from the Holy Spirit for this church."

"I was momentarily stunned," Buford remembers. "I had no idea who the woman was, and I couldn't believe she had the nerve to interrupt my sermon."

He recovered and said in a forceful voice, "No, ma'am. Please be seated."

She sat down, but after a moment, she stood again and said, "I feel compelled to give this congregation a message from the Holy Spirit."

"Now I was angry," Buford says. "First of all, if the Holy Spirit wants to say something to me or you, why can't He go direct? Why tell somebody else to tell me? Secondly, she was messing with about ten hours of good hard sermon preparation. I got very close to the microphone and yelled, 'Sit down and shut up!'"

The woman sat down, and a rattled Buford quickly ended his sermon.

After the service, another church member approached Buford and told him who the woman was. She was the wife of a high-powered attorney. In fact, the man's firm handled all the business for Clayton County.

"I didn't sleep much that night," Buford remembers. "All I could think about was how much trouble that woman's husband could cause for me and the church."

The next morning, his assistant walked into his office and said in a small voice, "The county attorney is on the phone for you."

"My hands were trembling when I picked up the phone. I almost started with a profuse apology, but instead I composed myself and said, 'Hello, Mr. King.'"

"I understand my wife was in your service yesterday," King began.

"Yes, sir."

"I also understand she stood up in the middle of your sermon and tried to speak to the congregation."

"Yes, sir."

"I also understand that you told her to 'sit down and shut up.' Is that true?"

"Yes, sir."

"Well, did she?"

"Yes, sir."

After a long pause, King said, "Would you mind telling me how you did that?"

My father was always on the lookout for a good sermon illustration. In the early 1980s, God gave him the greatest one of all time. It was an epic illustration of Galatians 6:7 and 8, a verse that is usually shortened into, "We reap what we sow." The King James Version goes like this: "Be not deceived; God is not mocked: for whatsoever a man soweth, that shall he also reap. For he that soweth to his flesh shall of the flesh reap corruption; but he that soweth to the Spirit shall of the Spirit reap life everlasting." One spring, Dad sowed squash – lots of it – and he reaped a harvest large enough to feed the five thousand.

According to the Environmental Protection Agency's current website, "Thirty years ago, thousands of American cities dumped their raw sewage directly into our nation's rivers, lakes, and bays. Today, because of improved wastewater treatment, our waterways have been cleaned up and made safer for recreation and seafood harvest." They are referring to a process in which wastewater is treated and recycled for use as fertilizer.

What the website doesn't say is that some municipalities have been turning waste into fertilizer since the early 1980s. Clayton County, Georgia, was one of them. Back then, the treated solids were called sludge. Now the products are euphemistically referred to as "biosolids," and that renamed sludge is no longer free. A bag of GroCo (a compost mixture of sawdust and Washington State biosolids called "Loop") costs around $5. A dump truck load large enough to spread the product one inch deep over an acre would cost over $4,000.

My parents, together with five other families in the church, purchased a large piece of land in 1979 and divided it into five-acre lots. To build the roads and grade the lots for construction, the families pooled their money and purchased a used bulldozer and an ancient dump truck. I was thirteen when we moved into our new home on Hebron Way in Ellenwood, Georgia. My aunt and uncle and cousins lived just up the hill from us. Charles Swift (Swifty) and Arnette, who had spent the previous decade being transferred by Gulf Oil to England, Virginia, and Texas, were back in Atlanta, and they lived next door. My grandparents owned the lot on the other side of the Swifts.

Dad had begun dreaming of a place with acreage the day he came home from work to find his backyard garden destroyed by bulldozers grading the lot behind us to construct a new house. So after we were settled in our new home, and after he'd gotten a Southern landscape of emerald green fescue, azaleas, and wild dogwoods established, he was ready to put in a garden.

If I close my eyes, I can still see Dad struggling with the old tiller he'd bought from my granddad. He turned up that red Georgia clay and made neat rows in the acre behind the peach trees, blueberry bushes, and grape vines he'd already planted. I see mom bent over, a roll of twine in her hands, helping him mark the rows. And I remember dropping seeds into the ground – lima beans, cantaloupes, and squash. Dad was crazy about squash because it had always been one of his top producers. The year he fed the multitude, he'd ordered every variety of squash seed in the Burpee catalog, twenty-three in all.

By the time I was old enough to date, dad's garden was supplying most of the fruits and vegetables we ate. My maternal

In the Garden

grandfather was a cattle farmer, and his cows and chickens were the source of our meat and fresh eggs. I have little difficulty believing that the excellent health I enjoy in my forties is due to that grass-fed meat, free-range chickens and their eggs, and organic produce, the kind of food for which we pay a premium these days.

Dad was, of necessity, an organic gardener. He was supporting a stay-at-home wife and three kids on a preacher's salary, and money was tight. In the spring of 1983, he read about a free fertilizer program in the newspaper. The waste treatment plant in our county was processing human waste into pellets. The product, called sludge, was free to county residents willing to take it. One Friday morning, he took the old neighborhood dump truck to the waste treatment plant and filled it to the top with that free fertilizer. He hauled the load back to our house and carefully backed the dump truck into a space between the fruit trees and the garden. But when he pushed the button that would raise the lift and dump the load of pellets, nothing happened. The lift on that old truck had died. There was no way for him to spread it over the garden unless he shoveled it out by hand.

He began shoveling, but it started raining hard, enough to make Noah nervous. Dad was forced into the house to wait until the rain stopped.

It was still pouring when I got home from school that afternoon. I parked my car as close to the carport as possible and ran inside. Mom was in the kitchen beginning dinner. "What's the dump truck doing in the yard?" I asked. Our five acres was pie-shaped, so the fruit trees and garden sat to the side of the house and were easily visible from the street. The dump truck was situated about ten feet from the edge of our gravel driveway.

"Your dad got a load of sludge for the garden today, but the lift's broken. He has to get Swifty to fix it before he can dump it out," Mom said.

"Sludge? What's that?'

She just smiled and said, "Ask your dad."

When the entire family was gathered around the dinner table, and after my little sister, Holly, said the fastest blessing on the planet– "ThankYouforthefoodamen" – I asked my dad why the dump truck was in our yard.

It was fertilizer, he said, explaining that the waste treatment plant had a new process for treating raw sewage to sanitize it, kill the bacteria, and eliminate most of the smell.

All I heard was waste treatment plant.

"You mean it's poop?"

"Yeah, but it's sanitized," he insisted. "And in that pellet form, with all the moisture removed from it, it doesn't smell."

"Um, there's a little moisture being added back to it," my brother, who was fourteen, reminded everyone.

"Daaaaad, the prom is tomorrow night." It came out as a wail.

As my whole family sat around the dinner table laughing at my pain, I could see a sermon illustration forming in my dad's brain, something about everything in our lives being fertilizer. *Yes, it may stink at first, but God can use the most sordid circumstances to bring forth a beautiful harvest.*

"Don't worry," he said. "I'll have it all spread by the time Roger comes to pick you up."

The next morning, Dad walked next door and asked Swifty to have a look at the lift. Swifty came over, sniffed the air, and whipped a red bandanna out of his back pocket to tie over his nose and mouth. After a couple of hours, he managed to get the lift working. Dad stood next to the dump truck holding a shovel

In the Garden

as the lift slowly pushed the front edge of the bed into the air. Swifty pushed the button that opened the gate. Nothing happened for a minute. Then the re-hydrated load of pellets slowly slid out in one massive dump-truck-bed shaped pile.

I'd gone to pick up Roger's boutonniere. When I pulled into the driveway and saw that massive pile of poop in our yard, I looked to the heavens and said, "Jesus, today would be a good day for the Rapture to happen." That, or maybe the earth could open up and just swallow me whole. I was pretty sure my life was over.

My brother was standing in the kitchen when I walked inside. He saw my face and burst out laughing. "Don't worry. It's sanitized," he said.

True to his word, my dad shoveled that sludge all afternoon. By six o'clock, when Roger was scheduled to pick me up, that pile had been reduced to the size of two toppled port-a-potties.

Swifty brought his tractor over and plowed that natural fertilizer into that hard Georgia clay. A healthy dose of spring showers followed, and the results were nothing short of miraculous. Dad's garden produced so much crooked-neck squash that summer that he took to filling the trunk of his car with it every Sunday night and begging parishioners to take as much as they wanted. There were jokes about how Jesus fed five thousand with twelve loaves of bread and two fish, but my father fed an entire congregation off of ten dollars' worth of squash seeds and free sludge.

As a plus, he harvested nearly as many sermon illustrations as he did squash. One was this: *you always reap later than you sow, and you always reap more than you sow.* The garden certainly proved that point! I also think that garden gave him something he didn't often receive from his day job at the church. It produced tangible results of his hard work in a relatively short period of time.

Mom figured out how to incorporate squash into every meal – zucchini bread for breakfast, squash pickles for lunch, or pureed and added to dinner's spaghetti sauce and meatloaf. She canned so much squash the pantry's wooden shelves sagged in the middle. And we ate so much squash that summer – twenty-three different kinds – that I remember thinking that I'd have to live to ninety before I could ever look at a crook-neck squash again.

There Shall Be Showers of Blessing

There shall be showers of blessing:
This is the promise of love[18]

Of course, visitation and sermon preparation are only two of a pastor's jobs. Finding ways to attract new congregants is a huge one, for as the old adage goes, "Anything that isn't growing is dying."[19] Promoting the church and its programs was definitely one of Buford's strengths. Perhaps it was a bit of hardheadedness that allowed him to ignore the insults and insinuations of other pastors who derided him for the Halloween Trail or an Easter egg hunt. Maybe it was just that he was a young man on a mission, confident that he was doing the Lord's work. Either way, he carried on, dreaming up innovative ways to attract crowds. But sometimes, they were more trouble than they were worth.

Sometime in early 1976, Buford realized that July 4, the Bicentennial anniversary of the United States, would fall on a Sunday. "And it dawned on me that the nation's 200th birthday falling on a Sunday was providential for our church. I thought the timing was perfect for us to make a big deal out of the day," he

---

18 Written by Daniel W. Whittle; based on Ezekiel 34:26
19 Especially a church!

says. The church hired a well-known Gospel singer named Doug Oldham to perform a complete concert. They rented the county's high school football stadium, Tara Stadium, (named for the plantation in Margaret Mitchell's *Gone With the Wind*, which was set in nearby Jonesboro, Georgia), and offered a free barbeque chicken dinner with all the trimmings to everyone who came. The church bought radio ads and blanketed the county with mailings and posters and flyers in every neighborhood. The event was advertised as a patriotic service with a free concert and a free dinner on Sunday morning, July 4, 1976. It was a tremendous undertaking, and 10,000 people were expected to attend. Several men in the church constructed a special stage for the center of the stadium field. Dozens of church members helped with publicity. Hundreds worked through the night of July 3 assembling the chicken dinners – 10,000 barbequed chickens with beans and slaw in Styrofoam containers. Sound equipment was set out the night before, and Doug Oldham and his crew showed up for a brief rehearsal.

In 1976, there was no live Doppler radar. And there were no ten-day forecasts. Buford says, "I woke up at about 4:00 that Sunday morning to the sound of heavy rain, what Southerners call a frog choker. It was as if God Himself had conspired against us. I was flabbergasted that we'd done everything we could do and God was letting us down. I thought maybe it would stop in time for the service. It did lighten up, but the skies were threatening. Right around the time the service started, a deluge of epic proportions began. We scrambled to cover the sound equipment. People ran for the exits. Those stacks of Styrofoam containers of chicken dinners were drowned."

It was a disaster. The church had spent tens of thousands of dollars, and members had worked heroically, all to no avail. Doug

Oldham took pity on the church. In a gallant gesture, he said he wanted to be part of the sacrifice, and he reduced his fee by half.

"I remember getting into my car and just driving so that I could collect my thoughts. I wondered why God had failed us. My wife was concerned for me. No one could find me, and people began wondering if I'd killed myself," Buford says.

The lesson? Maybe it's that we can work and plan and strategize, but ultimately, we have to acknowledge that only God is in complete control.

Perhaps it's that what we consider a disaster can be another's good fortune. That afternoon, thousands of those chicken dinners were distributed to homeless shelters and food banks across the Atlanta area.

Or maybe it's just that sometimes we need to learn not to take ourselves so seriously.

One thing is for sure, though: no one who was a member of the church on July 4, 1976, will ever forget that day.

I was nine on July 4, 1976, and that day was the first time I'd ever been in Tara Stadium. I sat with all the kids from Super Church. Most likely, our parents were busy with preparations that morning and this was the church's form of childcare for its volunteers.

I remember sitting toward the top of the stadium's south side right around the fifty-yard line. I'd heard adults discuss rain, but I don't think I was particularly concerned. What did worry me was the fact that there weren't many people in the stands. Even as a child, I knew how important this event was.

Everyone sang a hymn or two. I can't be sure, but I think we sang "My Country 'Tis of Thee" and "The Battle Hymn of the

Republic." Doug Oldham took the stage and began to sing. He was a big man, with a big, booming voice, and he was wonderful. But then it started raining the kind of rain that tells you it's time to abandon your plans, and everyone started running for cover.

Tara Stadium offered no shelter except for the bathrooms. We huddled under the eaves next to the bathroom's outside walls, soaked, waiting for our parents to claim us, and this image is forever burned into my brain: stacks of Styrofoam containers taller than I was sitting forlornly in the rain, water beading on their surfaces.

Doug Oldham went on to be a regular on Bill Gaither's specials and on Jerry Falwell's "Old Time Gospel Hour." Flipping channels as kids, we often saw him on television, and we never missed a chance to tease Dad about Doug and the Great Fourth of July Chicken Dinner Debacle.

My mom keeps a plastic bin full of old mementos and letters. In it, I found several "tickets" to the Bicentennial Worship Service. They were red, white, and blue, a tiny version of the Stars and Stripes with all the pertinent information about the event. At the very bottom, in tiny print, were these words: "In event of overflow crowds, seats cannot be guaranteed." When I pointed that sentence out to my dad, he shrugged and said, "You had to think big."

Just a Closer Walk with Thee

Just a closer walk with Thee,
Grant it, Jesus, is my plea.
Daily walking close to Thee,
Let it be, dear Lord, let it be[20]

That Fourth of July fiasco didn't deter Buford or the church leadership from their vision. Neither did it discourage them from dreaming up creative ways to attract new people to church. For instance, ask anyone who was a member of Clayton Community Church during the mid-1970s if they know what a Tuit is, and they'll probably chuckle. The church ordered hundreds of circular wooden chips stamped with the words "TUIT -- CLAYTON COMMUNITY CHURCH." On the flip side, the chip read, "I'll come to church when I get A ROUND TUIT." Those "Round Tuits" were distributed to all church members as a way of helping invite people to church.

Buford came up with a slogan for a bumper sticker that church members displayed on their cars for many years. The stickers were a bright royal blue with the words "I AM LOVED at Clayton Community Church" in white. It was a great slogan, for who

---

20 Author anonymous

doesn't want to be in a place where they feel loved? More than once, Buford mentioned from the pulpit that church members needed to take care to be polite drivers because they were advertising for Jesus and the church.[21]

Clayton Community continued to grow steadily throughout the next few years, adding various new ministries -- a missions program, a seniors' ministry, both men's and ladies' ministries – and increasing in both membership and weekly attendance. From January 1974 to January 1977, church offerings tripled. The school was consistently attracting new students, and in 1979, it celebrated its first graduating class.

Growth meant that space was, once again, at a premium. During the spring of 1976, the Board of Elders discussed the church's options. There was a tract of land, thirty-five acres, for sale on Mt. Zion Boulevard at a price of $175,000. Another twenty-five acres on the same road was on the market for $162,000. Judge Alvin Foster owned a recreational property named Indian Lake that he wanted to sell. At seventy acres, it was twice the size of the other two properties, and he was willing to sell it for $175,000.[22]

The fourth option was to stay on Reynolds Road. Between the church building and Reynolds Road was an area that was

---

21 In researching for this book, one of my favorite quotes was from Amie Berry Rush, who told me she remembered her great-grandmother, known to everyone in the church as Granny Berry, proudly displaying that bumper sticker on her little white Mustang. Amy says, "She proudly advertised her love for her church while also yelling in fits of road rage at most people driving in Clayton County." *Mustang Granny, think you better slow that Mustang down.*

22 Indian Lake remained in the Foster family until 1991. Renamed Atlanta Beach Sports and Entertainment Park, it was sold to Clayton County in 1995. The 1996 Olympic beach volleyball competition was held there.

two or three feet under water when it rained. Willows and scrubby bushes that thrive in a swampy area filled it. The City Council of Morrow had issued the church a building permit for the spot,[23] and Clayton County had given the church permission to move a sewer line in order to have room for the building. The only remaining obstacle was that they would be losing a parking lot. There was ample space behind the Ranch building, but it was under a power easement. The church asked Georgia Power for permission to construct a parking lot under that easement, and Georgia Power gave their consent. Only then did the Elders vote unanimously to stay at 5900 Reynolds Road and to build a new auditorium on that swampy patch of ground.

That summer, Buford and a group of volunteers took chainsaws to the entire area, leaving everything where it was cut. Then they hired someone to move the remaining dirt from the hill under the power lines to fill in the swampy area. About three or four feet of that fill dirt was placed over the area that had been clear-cut, and that's where the third building on the property went. To do it, the builder used a floating slab. The footings of that building were extra wide, maybe several times the normal size, and were tied to the concrete slab, making the whole thing kind of sit on top of the fill dirt.

To raise money for this new building, the church once again issued bonds, this time raising $700,000 for the project. Plans called for a 1,200-seat auditorium surrounded by four hallways of classrooms that would be used as school classrooms during the week and Sunday school rooms on Sundays. Stairwells

---

23 It wasn't until 1989 that the Georgia Planning Act was passed, giving the Department of Natural Resources the authority to dictate the standards for wetlands protection in local land use plans.

were located in the four corners of the building. The surrounding hallways were each painted a different color – blue and gold on the main floor, green and orange on the second level. Odd numbered rooms were on the north side of the building, which was closest to the parking lot, and even numbers were located on the south side. People were directed to the rooms they sought by color – "Room 204 will be upstairs in the orange hall. Go through the foyer to the stairwell, and you'll find the room on your right as you proceed down that hallway."

The classroom part was completed in time for the 1977-78 school year to begin, but the auditorium remained unfinished. It was used as a school gym until 1980, when the space was renovated into an auditorium at the cost of approximately $135,000.

Having a large part of the building unfinished while hundreds of school children came and went every day would not be permitted today, and for good reason. Along the upperlevel back hallway of the new building was a hole where the auditorium's baptistry would be placed once the auditorium was finished. Junior- and senior-high school students successfully navigated that back hallway every day. Early one morning, however, an elementary teacher unfamiliar with that hall attempted to walk it in the dark. She fell into the baptistry hole and broke her leg. The school paid her medical bills, of course, and after that, the hole was carefully covered.

Not long after the auditorium (along with its new baptistry) was completed, a group of ten or twelve women from Morrow Methodist Church, which was right around the corner, called Buford and asked him if he would be willing to baptize them. They had already been baptized in the Methodist church by sprinkling but had somehow become convinced that form of baptism was invalid. It was January, and Buford warned them that it was not an ideal time for baptism, but they were adamant, so he agreed. The new baptistry was supposedly a heated one, but when Buford arrived about an hour before that Sunday evening service, the water was, in his words, "roughly the temperature of those highway grocery store ice chests where you stuck your hand in to grab a Coca Cola." When the Methodist ladies arrived, he explained the situation, but they insisted on going through with it. Buford wore waders when he baptized, so he was partially insulated from the cold water, but he says, "As I walked into the baptistry, I could feel the temperature of the water through the waders, and I knew it was going to be painful for those ladies. I remember each one of the women catching her breath as she entered the water, then trembling furiously as she exited. They were blue when they came up out of the water."

As nice as it was, there was one drawback to the new auditorium; it came at the expense of the school gym. The Christian school's indoor sports – girls' volleyball and girls' and boys' basketball – had to be played in a rented gym. Students were bused to a church gym near the Moreland Avenue exit off of I-285 for practice for the next school year.

Although the property seemed to be built out, enough space was available to squeeze in a gymnasium at an angle between the Ranch building, the first church building, and the creek, with only about ten feet between a back corner of the building and that creek.[24] A building fund drive raised $100,000 for construction, and the school opened the 1981-82 school year with a new gym.

Further expansion was impossible on the site, so Buford approached Judge Reynolds, who was by this time in his eighties,

---

24 Thereby giving an extra layer of meaning to the old saying, "Lord willing and the creek don't rise."

about selling a portion of his property to the church. In 1976, Reynolds donated 130 acres across the street from the church to Clayton County, and to this day, it is a nature preserve bearing his name. He still owned close to thirty acres on the same side of the road as the church, at the corner of Huie and Reynolds Roads. Although he had softened even more toward the church over the years, he still adamantly refused to sell his land to "that crazy bunch down in the swamp." Judge Alvin Foster, the same man who donated the money to start the Christian school, was finally able to persuade Reynolds to sell him the twenty-nine acres. And after Reynolds' death, the church purchased it from Foster for approximately $150,000.

The year the "big" building was completed, I was in sixth grade. Most of my classes were in the green hall, which was upstairs and faced out toward the parking lot. I remember sitting in class every morning and watching my dad trudge across the parking lot with a large Styrofoam cup of coffee in one hand and his Bible in the other. Once he'd crossed the parking lot and climbed the hill where the large towers of power lines sat, he would cross Reynolds Road and disappear into the woods of Reynolds Park. Dad went to the nature preserve every day of the week to escape the barrage of telephone calls and meetings so that he could, as he put it, "talk to God."

One of the classes I had in that green hall room was Bible class. No Bible teacher at CCS ever went more than a few days without reminding us students of the importance of daily devotions. I don't know if any of my classmates ever noticed, but Dad was setting the example.

I always thought those hours in the woods must have been more about God talking to my dad, because he always seemed to know exactly how to handle everything. I realize this is the opinion of a devoted daddy's girl, but, simply put, my dad was perfect. As I remember things, he always knew best. I was stunned to find out that not everyone felt the same way.

How Great Thou Art

Then sings my soul, my Savior, God, to thee
How great thou art! How great thou art![25]

By the time the church was ten years old, it was pretty clear that Buford Adams was the senior pastor for the long haul, although he liked to joke that he was still praying for the permanent pastor to show up. The church and all of its ministries were growing and, for the most part, running smoothly. Under the direction of Bob Nama, the AWANA program (charter 1620) had grown to be the biggest club in the state of Georgia. Church finances were sound.

The staff's weekly schedule centered around Sunday services: Mondays, the finance office counted the offering, and the front office mailed letters thanking visitors for being at church the day before and new member packets to those who had joined the church; Tuesdays began with staff meeting and a deadline for submissions to the weekly bulletin because the paste-up was due at the printer's on Wednesday; sometime on Wednesday or Thursday, the music minister[26] would submit an order of service

---

25 HOW GREAT THOU ART by Stuart K. Hine
© 1949, 1953 The Stuart Hine Trust. Used by permission of Hope Publishing Company, Carol Stream, IL 60188.
26 Charlie Murphey filled the position from approximately 1980 to '86

complete with the hymn selections and the names of those performing special music to Buford for his approval.

Buford was the type of leader who wanted to tell people what he expected and then leave them alone to do the job. He wasn't interested in micro-managing, but the one thing he insisted on over-planning and being meticulously prepared for was the Sunday morning service. No one but he or the associate pastor gave announcements because some people are unpredictable when handed a microphone. Musicians were forbidden from speaking "just a few words" about the song they were going to perform. In short, no one opened his or her mouth on stage during that hour-long worship service unless the words had been pre-approved.

The order of service every Sunday morning went something like this:

Opening Hymn
Prayer
Another congregational hymn
Welcome from one of the pastors, who would give one or two very brief announcements
Choir Special
Congregational hymn
Special music
Message
Invitation and Introduction of New Members
Closing Hymn -- always the chorus of "How Great Thou Art"[27]

---

27 In 2001, this song was voted the second-most loved hymn of all time (after "Amazing Grace"). During the 1950s, it became popular as the signature song of the Billy Graham Crusades. It has been recorded over 1,700 times, and in 1967, Elvis Presley won a Grammy for his performance of the song.

I Am Loved at Community Bible Church

Around the time the church moved into the big building on Reynolds Road, someone stuck a cartoon outside of Buford's office door. It depicted a man whose hind end had a huge chunk bitten out of it. The caption read, "Nothing serious, just a little chat with the boss." It hung there for probably fifteen years.

In 1970, when the church started, Buford borrowed a copy of the constitution governing Grove Community Church in Miami, Florida, the church Babs had attended as a teenager, to use as a model for Clayton Community. There are basically three possibilities for governing a church. There is a congregational-led church, which is like Baptist churches, where the membership votes on every issue. The problem is that large floor fights can erupt when people disagree. There is a session-led church, which is one in which a small group, perhaps called Elders, are the governing body of the church. Or there are the churches run from the top down, like the Catholic or Episcopalian churches or the Church of God, with a whole structure of individuals above the church so that the denomination as a whole dictates what the individual churches will do. The session-led model had worked well for Grove Community, and Buford wanted a similar church government.

"Bob Kohl and I sat down and studied that constitution and made a few changes, not a whole lot. I didn't want a Baptist congregational type of government. I'd seen too many church fights where you have a business meeting where everyone's yelling at one another, and I didn't want a completely top down government like Episcopalian or Catholic. We wanted some sort of government that was responsive to the members, so we chose a session-led group of individuals who would be the church government." That body of leaders was called the Board of Elders.

While he shouldered the responsibility for the daily operations of the church, Buford had intentionally dis-involved himself from the finances of the church, turning them over to the finance committee. Most of the people on that committee were not involved in the day-to-day operations but were making the financial decisions for the church, and there began to be some conflict. Buford remembers, "There was a particular strand of theology at the time that believed churches shouldn't be pastored by one person but by a group of elders who were totally equal. No one person should be dominant in the group, and the pastorate should be a group enterprise. I disagreed with that, and we had a gentlemanly discussion along theological lines that lasted for about two years. They had verses saying there should be equality of elders, and I had my verses arguing that the church should be pastored by an individual. At some point, it became a more spirited argument."

At that time, Jack Bartlett was living about an hour away, in Woodstock, where he pastored a church. Buford would occasionally drive up to have a cup of coffee with him and discuss the situation. Jack explains, "It was couched in the question of do the Elders run the church or does the pastor, but it really came down to two men and which of those two dominant personalities was going to run it."

Part of the problem was that one of those dominant personalities was the church's biggest financial contributor. Buford was the other.

It came to a head in 1982. One Sunday after the evening service, in a specially-called meeting, Buford told the Board of Elders that he could not be the pastor if he wasn't the one leading the church. "I said that as senior pastor, I've got to be able to lead the church and be the senior pastor. If there's ever a majority of the Elders who believe I shouldn't be pastor, I'm going to give you the right to dismiss me. But if I had the majority vote of the Board of

Elders, I intended to lead the church." He insisted that they take a vote, not knowing which way it would come out.

Buford won. He immediately asked the other man to resign his position on the Board of Elders.

Jack Bartlett shakes his head at the memory. "That whole situation showed that everyone has a good side and an ugly one. And a lot of ugly sides came out that night."

As a result, about one hundred people left the church and formed a congregation in the southern part of Clayton County. The group included some of the church's biggest givers, the head of children's ministries, and much of the church leadership. "I wondered what it was going to do to us and how we'd survive without those folks," Buford admits, but says that, looking back on it, both congregations have continued to grow. "So in essence, we just spawned another church."

The church constitution has been revised only two times in its history, and they were minor revisions. The first time was after the split. "We went back to the constitution and changed it so that the Board of Elders, if they ever deemed me or any other pastor unfit for service -- if we committed adultery or preached heresy or stole money from the church, egregious things -- they could get rid of that pastor with a majority vote by the Board of Elders," Buford says, acknowledging that it was a sort of compromise with the group insisting on a plurality of pastors.

He continues, "I think it (the church constitution) has worked so well because we've kind of ignored it. We've had very few issues that have come to a congregational decision. If the church enters into real debt, there has to be a congregational vote for that. Or if we call a new senior pastor. Basically, though, the constitution is on a shelf and we don't pass it around, don't talk about it, and only a very detailed person who is a stickler for that kind of stuff ever bothers to ask about it. When you get into the exact words and start arguing over this paragraph or that paragraph, then you get into real trouble."

Buford waited for a year after the split to see how the church's membership and finances would level out. Then, in early 1984, he called Jack Bartlett and asked him to consider moving back to Clayton County to be his associate pastor.

Jack recalls, "Pastoring that church in Woodstock was preparation for everything else in my life. I learned a lot about church, and I learned a lot about people. I had this naïve idea that I was going to go up there and love everybody and everybody was going to love me. It was a big wakeup call to realize that everybody don't love me and everyone doesn't want to do it my way." He chuckles and then says, "The biggest thing, though, was I learned about me. I learned who I was and who I wasn't. I learned I wasn't Buford Adams. It was a sweet day when I realized that that's okay, that I can fit into a different kind of ministry slot. I wasn't a quarterback, but I could be a good halfback. I could still score points." Jack and his wife, Diana, and their twin daughters, Lisa and Laurie, moved back to Clayton County, and he stepped into that position in the summer of 1984, taking over some of the pastoral duties for which he was well-suited – hospital visits, pastoral care, and, perhaps most helpful to Buford, preaching the Sunday evening services.

Around the time Jack Bartlett was learning that not everyone necessarily agreed with the way he did things, I was a high school junior coming to the realization that although I thought my dad was perfect, not everyone shared that belief. It happens in every kid's life, to be sure, but my version of that important life lesson was learned in a fairly public arena, and it changed the course of my life.

Mom and Dad were careful about how much Beau, Holly, and I knew about the situation. They could control what we found out from them. But what they couldn't control was what other people said to me at school and at youth ministry meetings. Once, a fellow student lashed out at me during volleyball practice: "Your dad doesn't own this place!"

I remember thinking, *No, he doesn't. But you haven't seen all the blood, sweat, and tears he's put into it. I have, and I know that no one loves it like he does.*

When the split officially happened, and those who left started a new church in Fayetteville, I took to calling them the "Fayette-villains." I was an angry girl, and the lasting effect it had on me was this: I had always seen myself as following in my parents' footsteps and somehow being in ministry, most likely married to a man who pastored a church. But what I came to learn about myself was that I was pretty tough when it came to ignoring others' criticism of me. Sideways glances didn't stick; they rolled off me like beads of water on a freshly waxed car. But if you say something about someone I love, especially my daddy, I will bite. And I will never let it go. That church split was the beginning of my realization that I'm much too onion-skinned for ministry.

The funny thing about the church split is that Dad and the man who challenged him are now good friends. It's a credit to both, I think, that they came away from it able to learn about themselves, able to see themselves in a new light. Dad became a softer version of himself, more willing to listen, and more willing than ever to learn.

Standing on the Promises

Standing on the promises, I cannot fall,
Listening every moment to the Spirit's call,
Resting in my Savior as my all in all,
Standing on the promises of God[28]

Almost everyone who regularly stands before a crowd and speaks will admit to feeling relief on days when they don't have to prepare something to say. Teachers, for instance, rarely turn down an opportunity to show a quality video or a TedTalk as a means of illustrating a point they're trying to make. Pastors need breaks, and those often come in the form of guest speakers.

Buford never was much for guest speakers, but not because he pined for the pulpit. He never relinquished the prime Sunday morning worship service slots to anyone who wasn't thoroughly vetted. Consequently, the list of guest speakers at the church during his tenure as senior pastor was very short.

One of the church's few guest speakers in the early 1970s was a man named Charles "Tremendous" Jones. Jones was a former insurance salesman who made it his mission to help people improve their lives by reading. In 1965, he started Life Management Services, a consulting firm that today would be described as life coaching. He became a famous motivational speaker and was the

---

28 Words and music by Russell Kelso Carter

author of several books, including *Life Is Tremendous*. He died in 2008, but he will forever be remembered for this famous quote: "You are the same today as you'll be in five years except for two things: the books you read and the people you meet."

Dr. Dolphus Weary stood in the church's pulpit in the early 1980s. A native of rural Mississippi, he was one of the first African-American students to attend the all-white Los Angeles Baptist College. He graduated in 1969 with a B.S. in Biology. Weary then earned a master's degree in Religious Education from Los Angeles Baptist Seminary and then returned to Mississippi, where he earned his M.Ed. from the University of Southern Mississippi. He went to work for a Christian organization named Mendenhall Ministries, where he served from 1971 until 1997. He would later receive a Doctor of Ministry from Reformed Theological Seminary in Jackson, Mississippi. It was during his time at Mendenhall that Weary began traveling across the United States, delivering a message of racial reconciliation: "I believe that God has given me two passions; a passion for racial unity in the Body of Christ and to minister to those who are poor in Mississippi and around the country." Weary would have a lasting impact on the church.

Only one guest speaker, though, was a regular over the years. His name was Major Ian Thomas.

Major Thomas was an English citizen who served in the British Expeditionary Forces. At the beginning of World War Two, he participated in Operation Dynamo, the code name for the evacuation of Allied troops from Dunkirk, France, between May 27 and June 4, 1940, after thousands of British, French, and Belgian troops were cut off and surrounded by the German army during the Battle of France. Over 345,000 men were rescued by 800 boats during the evacuation.

In 1947, Major Thomas and his wife, Joan, decided to combat the devastation of World War Two by opening their home to young people. He had special concern for German youth who had been displaced by the war, and he helped many of them go to England, where he gave them a place to live and educated them. Thomas purchased a place that would serve as headquarters for his ministry, Capernwray Hall, which began as a place that offered food and shelter. The German students called themselves "Fackeltraeger," meaning "carriers of the torch." Eventually, Bible schools based on the Capernwray model began springing up around Europe, and "Torchbearers" became the official name of Thomas' ministry.

Over the next two decades, Thomas authored several books, the most notable of which was *The Saving Life of Christ*, and he became a popular speaker at churches in Europe, the United States, and Australia. Buford read *The Saving Life of Christ* and wrote a letter inviting Thomas to speak at the church.

Because Major Thomas was booked nearly two years in advance, and because he traveled from so far to speak at the church, his visits would often resemble an old-time revival. He would speak at both Sunday morning and evening services, then continue with evening meetings through the next week. His conferences ended on Friday night, and he used Saturdays to travel to his next speaking engagement.

Major Thomas made it known to the churches hosting him that he preferred to stay in the home of the pastor's family rather than in a hotel. He always traveled with a protégé, a young man in his early twenties who was studying at one of the Torchbearers schools, who acted as his assistant. The two traveled light – one suitcase each, a briefcase full of Major Thomas' papers, and an old manual typewriter on which Major Thomas would type his own correspondence.

During the 1980s, he was a guest at the church three times. In the fall of 1984, he became ill during the course of the week's conference and collapsed while speaking. He was rushed to the hospital, where doctors diagnosed him with phlebitis, an inflammation of the veins in his legs. He spent two days in the hospital, then recovered at the Adams' house for the next two weeks.

I was a freshman away at college when Major Thomas spent two weeks recuperating at my parents' house, so I didn't get to know him as well as my younger brother and sister did. Instead, I have only two memories of Major Thomas's visits to our home. The first is simply a mental picture of him sitting in our kitchen in front of his old typewriter. He had lost his right index finger just above the knuckle in battle, and he pecked at the keys using his left index finger and the nub of his right one.

My second memory is of a minor skirmish that took place between the Major and my mom. Mom took her job as pastor's wife very seriously. She made a career out of running the perfect family, and she was good at what she did. We were fed, perfectly groomed, and on time for every church service.

Mom believed that a hot, hearty breakfast is the best way to start the school day. That belief, plus the fact it was my dad's favorite breakfast, meant she cooked a large meal of fresh scrambled eggs from my grandmother's hens plus bacon or sausage, grits, and homemade biscuits Monday through Friday. Saturdays, we were on our own for breakfast, and that meant we were allowed a bowl of cold cereal – Cheerios or Raisin Bran, though, because refined sugar and flour were "not fit for human consumption." Every Sunday, my dad rose at 4:30 to prepare for the morning services. He showered, dressed, and left the house by five to go to the Waffle House for breakfast so that he could be at church by six – "cramming" for the morning message, we always teased. So Mom was left with getting us three children ready on Sunday mornings. Our breakfast on those days was cheese toast – a slice of wheat bread topped with a piece of real cheese (none of that processed mess!) broiled in the oven until the cheese bubbled. It was cheap, quick, and, in my opinion, a little slice of Heaven before church.

Major Thomas was speaking this particular Sunday morning. Dad was already at church, so it was Mom's job to get all of us kids plus the Major and his assistant to church on time. To Mom, it didn't matter if you were a nine-year-old girl who couldn't find her black patent Mary Janes or formerly in the Queen's service: making her late to church was an unpardonable sin. In fact, whenever I hear the phrase "Get me to the church on time," I don't picture a wedding. I picture my childhood. Sundays at nine o'clock sharp, Mom was gunning the engine of our powder-blue 1977 AMC Pacer.[29]

Mom called everyone to the breakfast table promptly at 8:45 that morning. When she set that slice of cheese toast in front of Major Thomas, he looked at it the way we Americans look at the pork and beans the British favor for breakfast. And then he watched us kids pick up our cheese toast with our fingers and eat it much like an Italian folds a slice of pizza. He attempted to pick his slice up, but it drooped over his fingers, and the cheese began sliding off the bread. He said to my mother in a slightly imperious tone, "I wonder, might one properly eat this with a knife and fork?"

---

29 It looked just like the car in the 1992 film *Wayne's World*, and of course, it sported one of the "I AM LOVED at Clayton Community Church" bumper stickers.

Rising from her seat at the table to grab the utensils he'd requested, she said impatiently, "One might. And one might also want to eat quickly because he's about to make us late for church."

Mom won her battle with the old British warrior. We were on time to church that morning.

His Eye is on the Sparrow

I sing because I'm happy; I sing because I'm free;
For His eye is on the sparrow,
and I know He watches me[30]

During the first two years of the 1980s, America was embroiled in the Iranian hostage crisis, a recession, runaway inflation, and a prime interest rate that hit 21.5 percent. By 1983, inflation had eased somewhat, and the country began a period of sustained economic growth. Atlanta, the international headquarters of Delta Airlines, Coca-Cola, and the nascent Home Depot, was becoming a major metropolitan city. Clayton Community Church was thriving. The school was growing -- every one of those five hundred desks Robert Rohm had purchased was in use. Attendance at Sunday school and worship services was higher than it had ever been. But the youth ministry was foundering.

Part of the problem was that the church had, in a sense, swallowed up the youth ministry. The Atlanta Youth Ranch no longer had its own facility. Teenagers were attending youth meetings on the campus of Clayton Community Church. Church leadership began talking about constructing a separate youth building on the twenty-nine acres purchased from Judge Foster.

---

30 Words by Civilla D. Martin

The other half of the equation was that the youth ministry needed a new leader. Toney Jones had left abruptly a few years earlier, leaving a hole that others had unsuccessfully attempted to fill. The man who held the job in 1981, Donny Hamrick, was good at building close relationships with a small group of teenagers and discipling them, but he seemed unable to attract a crowd at the large Thursday evening meetings. An incident at Christmas Camp in Gatlinburg, Tennessee, in December 1981 marked the beginning of the end of his tenure as Youth Ranch director.

Camp had ended, and everyone was boarding the buses for the trip home. Unfortunately, the loading process was cumbersome, and the group's estimated departure time had already come and gone. This, of course, was in the days before cell phones, and Hamrick knew parents would be sitting in the church parking lot waiting for their kids and getting nervous because the buses were late. In a moment of frustration, he stepped aboard the lead bus and said to its driver, Sammy Benton, "This bus leaves in five minutes. I don't care who is or is not on it. Are we clear?"

Sammy nodded and looked down at his watch to mark the beginning of the five-minute countdown. Precisely five minutes after Donny's verbal mandate, Sammy closed the door and pulled away from the hotel, the second bus and the van following behind him.

About half an hour outside of Gatlinburg, someone began looking for Donny. The bus and van drivers were using two-way radios to communicate with each other, and they quickly realized that their leader was missing.

Sammy says, "We didn't leave him on purpose. Everyone [in our bus] thought he was on the other bus. I do remember no one wanted to go back because it was his fault for missing the bus. Driving a bus on mountain roads is not fun."

His Eye is on the Sparrow

It took a while for Donny Hamrick to live that down. For Buford, it was a sign that the youth ministry needed new leadership.

Buford had always thought of youth ministry as his first calling, so he was pained to see it struggle, but he had another reason to push for its success – his two older children were quickly approaching their teenage years. He began earnestly looking for a charismatic young man who could attract crowds to the large Thursday evening youth meetings and also nurture a core group of leaders among the church's teenagers. In other words, he needed someone familiar with the old Youth Ranch model.

During the early years of the Youth Ranch, a teenage girl named Corinne Dennis had begged Buford to start a Ranch in North Atlanta. Her parents had offered their home as an initial meeting place, and Buford agreed to drive to Sandy Springs on Tuesday evenings to speak. The North Atlanta Youth Ranch had grown large enough to warrant its own director, and Buford had brought in a fellow named Mike Schaffer to run it. Schaffer introduced Buford to a young man named Vince Pinyard, who worked full-time as an EMT for Metro Ambulance Company in Atlanta and helped with the music at the North Atlanta Youth Ranch. Buford was impressed with the way Vince could entertain a crowd, and he asked the young man if he wanted to be in full-time ministry.

Vince came on staff in the summer of 1981. He and his wife, Suzy, immediately organized a trip to Panama City, Florida, with the teenagers who were already in the youth group. That group of nine or ten became the new Council, and they went back to their high schools in the fall of 1981 ready to invite their friends to the newest incarnation of the Atlanta Youth Ranch, which had been re-named Powerplay. Vince formed a band with Charlie

Murphey, the church's music minister, and Charley's wife, Sue, to provide the music for the Powerplay meetings.

It was the right recipe. That Christmas, at least one hundred teens went to Powerplay's Christmas Camp in Fontana, North Carolina. And by the following spring, attendance at weekly Powerplay meetings averaged over one hundred.

Church youth groups are perpetually attempting to raise money, and Powerplay was no different. In the first few months after Vince joined the church staff, he began looking for ways to help teenagers pay for camp. Someone mentioned to him that in the past, Halloween haunted houses and trails had been a gold mine. The majority of the nearly thirty acres the church had purchased from Judge Reynolds via Judge Foster were heavily forested, perfect for a haunted trail. Vince jumped on the idea.

The church Elders told him no, and the reason was a bit surprising, given the ministry's history. Halloween trails and Easter bunnies had always been ways of thinking outside of the church's walls to attract new families to the church and its ministries. But in the early 1980s, the fundamentalism that had become so popular in Christian circles – the same ideas the church had flirted with, then rejected – had resurfaced in a couple of ways.

In the late 1970s, an organization named the "Institute in Basic Youth Conflicts," which had been founded in the late sixties by a man named Bill Gothard, enjoyed incredible success by taking week-long live seminars on life principles taught by Gothard to major U.S. cities. For instance, Gothard brought the seminar to Atlanta every June, filling up the nearly 15,000-seat Omni arena. Buford and Babs took a group from the church to the seminar every year, a contingent large enough to win Gothard's prized chalk drawing (presented to the organization represented by the most people) for a couple of years. Gothard had a fundamentalist bent, to be sure. He taught, for example, that rock music – even Christian rock – had a "sensual" beat that would entice listeners into immorality. He spoke about the dangers of dating, espousing a form of "courting" that sounded like a holdover from colonial times. By the early eighties, his teachings had gotten downright weird. Cabbage Patch dolls were satanic, and Christian families should shun birth control and shoot for a "quiver full" of children in order to create a population boom of fundamentalists. To his credit, Buford balked at the Cabbage Patch and Quiver-Full teachings. Realizing that Gothard was overstepping the boundary of God's conviction in a believer's personal life, Buford discontinued the church's endorsement of the seminars.[31] But fundamentalism kept popping its head up like a carnival Whack-A-Mole game; the school sent home a form for students to sign declaring they would not listen to any form of rock music. Anyone not signing the form would be asked to leave the school. The outcry was so great – parents insisted that they, not the school, had the right to monitor their kids' music -- that the school rescinded its ban on rock music.

In late summer 1981, when Vince Pinyard asked the Board of Elders for permission to use the church's property to hold a fundraiser, a Halloween Trail of Terror, they were adamantly opposed to it. The church was enjoying a degree of esteem in the community at that point. No longer was it the upstart non-denominational group of ex-hippies who would do anything to attract a crowd. Clayton Community Church had established itself as a respectable

---

31 Gothard resigned from his position as president of the Institute in Basic Life Principles on March 7, 2014, after allegations of sexual harassment from thirty-four women who worked for the ministry and accusations of molestation from four women. He was also accused of failing to report incidences of child abuse. Source: *Washington Post*.

body of believers, and the church leaders intended to hang on to that reputation. To their minds, the Trail celebrated Halloween, which was associated with Satan and the Occult, and using it to raise money, no matter how worthy the cause, would do irreparable damage to the church's standing in the community.

Vince asked for a hearing before the Board of Elders. The meeting was set for the day after Labor Day. Vince took with him two or three teenagers, who did all of the talking. They recounted the history of the Atlanta Youth Ranch and the early days of the church, when, like the Apostle Paul taught, every means of reaching people for Christ was acceptable. "I have become all things to all people so that by all possible means I might save some" (I Corinthians 9:22, NIV). They argued Philippians 1:18 – ". . . The important thing is that in every way, whether from false motives or true, Christ is preached. . . ." The Elders voted to grant permission for Powerplay to sponsor a Trail of Terror with the provisions that no satanic or demonic elements be included in the production and that every customer would hear a brief presentation of the Gospel.

Preparing to open the trail in time for Halloween week, which was less than two months away, was a daunting task. Within days, volunteers were in the woods, hacking out a trail with machetes.

Planning meetings took place every week, and in those meetings, "scenes" were sketched out. The plan was for a guide dressed in a black robe and outfitted with a single flashlight to escort groups of ten through the wooded trail. Scenes included a giant rolling "rock," borrowed from the 1981 film *Raiders of the Lost Ark*, chasing people down a section of the trail. Bodies would emerge from shallow dirt graves. A caged wild man would break through his bars and "attack." A guillotine would be constructed. "Jason" would hack at various victims in a scene reminiscent of the *Friday the 13th* movie series, and ultimately bury his hatchet in some poor girl's chest. A giant maze would be built. There was to be a horrifying car crash scene with bloody victims hanging out of the wreckage. A swinging bridge was sketched out for the exit. And holes had to be dug in the ground for the *coup de grace*, a *Texas Chainsaw Massacre* scene in which two or three chainsaws (chains removed, of course) would be powered up just as a group progressed through a scattering of headless, limbless bodies in a small clearing close to the end of the Trail.

To accomplish the "decapitations," a couple of brave volunteers were buried each night up to their necks.[32] Even though people standing in line -- sometimes for hours -- knew that scene was coming because they could hear chainsaws starting up every few minutes, the feeling of a vibrating chainsaw hitting their leg always scared people silly.

Vince had access to a camper, and he parked it at the edge of the woods and basically lived at the trail during the weeks leading up to it. Amazingly, all that work was accomplished on time even though several people who worked to clear the trail came down with terrible cases of poison oak. The inaugural Reynolds woods Trail of Terror opened the weekend before Halloween in 1981.

Not long after they encountered the chainsaw scene, and right before the swinging bridge exit, a group on the trail would be instructed to sit on small benches in a small clearing. There they would be given a short Gospel presentation and invited to accept Jesus as their Savior. During the presentation, a person would

---

32 Because of the volume of customers served every night, these intrepid and longsuffering kids often worked four or five hours without a bathroom break because it was impossible to dig them out between scenes.

stand silently in front of a large sandbox drawing words in the sand. And at the end of the Gospel, he would splash a bit of gasoline on the sandbox and hold a torch to it to punctuate the warning about spending eternity in Hell, separated from God. If the purpose of the trail was, as some joked, to scare the Hell out of people, then this was an over-the-top way of making the point.

Most of those scenes lasted for the nearly ten years Powerplay had the trail. But two did not. One year, the parents of one teenager offered the use of a horse trained to "stop on a dime." A "headless" rider was instructed to gallop the horse straight toward each group coming through the trail, then stop as the group scattered in fear. After a few nights, it became obvious that it was only a matter of time before someone got hurt, and the Headless Horseman scene was cancelled. And in 1983, the third year of the trail, the teenager in charge of the final scene got carried away between groups one night. He was practicing with new words to write in the sand, and there was a delay between groups long enough that he wrote two or three different words, sprinkled the gasoline, then changed his mind and started over. By the time a new group of spectators was seated, there was enough gasoline in that sandbox to cause a huge fireball that singed the eyebrows of everyone on the front row. The flames spread to the trees above, and the entire trail had to be evacuated. Fortunately, the damage was minimal, and the show resumed after the local fire department gave the all clear that the fire had been extinguished. The only casualty was the Hell scene itself.

During the years Powerplay sponsored that trail, thousands of people lined up to pay for a trip through it. Vince says, "[This is] strictly a guess, but calculating ten in a group and six groups an hour (conservatively), with five hours a night, there were three hundred people per night, easily! With six nights each year, we had 1800 people a year, and again, those are conservative numbers." When all was said and done, the youth group earned enough money every year to pay for every teenager who worked most nights of the trail to attend Christmas camp in Fontana, North Carolina.

If Vince was good at eliciting an emotional response from teens during a Thursday night youth meeting, he was brilliant at it during a week of camp. Songs, skits, moving testimonies, guest speakers, and afternoon flag football games culminated in a final night dedication meeting. Over the years, hundreds of teenagers made life-changing decisions at Christmas camp, and in many instances, the Trail of Terror had been their ticket to camp.

In early 1984, Vince decided to finish his college education. He resigned from his position as Youth Minister effective that summer, and he and Suzy and their three children – Jeremy, Kelly, and Christie – moved to Kissimmee, Florida. Today, he is an emergency room physician in Johnson City, Tennessee.

Not long after Vince left, Charlie Murphey tendered his resignation. He and his wife, Sue, believed God was calling them to take their music ministry to the desert Southwest, so they moved with their children, Jamie and little Charlie, to Arizona. Steve and Denise Shivers, newlyweds who were both graduates of the prestigious Peabody Conservatory, had recently joined the church and were already serving in the music ministry as accompanists. Steve, who was a music professor at nearby Clayton Junior College, took the job of music minister on a temporary basis in 1988, thinking he would only be around for five or six years. Almost twenty-seven years later, Steve still leads the music in the traditional chapel service, and Denise teaches music at the school.

I Am Loved at Community Bible Church

Although my father had himself never quite fit the mold of a traditional youth minister, Vince managed to baffle even him in his first few months at the church. One day, Jack Bartlett heard gunshots on the church property. He walked outside to find Vince standing at the top of Ranch building's outdoor stairwell that faced the back parking lot. He had earplugs in his ears and was taking target practice in a church and school parking lot during school hours. I'm sure that at that point Dad and Jack wondered at the wisdom of hiring a pastor with a background as a paramedic. Then something happened to convince them that God had been in the decision to hire Vince Pinyard.

It was the spring of 1982, and Vince had been at the church less than a year. Several of the high school students were in the school office one morning when a parent walked in and said her car wouldn't start. She asked if someone would be willing to help jumpstart the car. Three boys – Marc Clark, Jeff Thiessen, and Marty Wyatt – ran to the student parking lot, which was behind the Ranch building, and brought Marc's car, a Volkswagen Beetle, around to help her. After they got the woman's car running, Jeff jumped on the running board of the car for the ride back to the student lot. Marty was driving, and when he took the sharp turn back into the car's parking spot, Jeff lost his grip on the car and was thrown off. He hit the asphalt head first.

Alan Parker was one of the young men in the school office when the mother asked for help starting her car, and he sprinted for the parking lot when Marc ran back to the school office screaming for someone to call for an ambulance. Alan says, "Vince's office and the Powerplay room looked out over that back parking lot. Vince heard the noise and the commotion and looked out his window, saw what had just taken place and ran outside to where Jeff was laying."

Jeff had gone into shock and was bleeding from his ear. He started seizing. Vince turned the young man on his side and administered appropriate care until an ambulance arrived.

Jeff had suffered a traumatic brain injury, and doctors weren't certain at first whether or not he would survive. Alan says, "I remember Jeff's mom and dad saying when I was at the hospital visiting Jeff a few days after the incident that the things Vince did for Jeff that day probably saved his life and kept it from being a worse situation."

We were scared until we got the news a couple of days later that Jeff was going to be okay. He never made it back to school that year, and he eventually repeated his entire senior year of high school at Forest Park Senior High.

Jeff's accident is my only bad memory from those years as a teenager at the church. I loved that youth group and the people in it, and I realize how lucky I was to spend my adolescent years in the safety and fun that ministry provided.

I was Dracula's victim during the first year of the Trail, and my boyfriend was Dracula (how lucky was that?). The next year, someone had the bright idea of renting an expensive gorilla costume, and somehow I was elected to be a not-so-very-scary 5'4" tall gorilla. My last year of high school, I worked in the ticket booth and arranged customers into the right-sized groups as they entered the trail.

My whole family was, in some way or another, involved in the trail. My dad stood out in the parking lot every night counting cars, estimating crowd size, directing traffic, and maintaining order. My mother, who would later earn a BFA in Fine Art as a portrait artist, did makeup. My brother, sister, and cousins all spent countless hours hanging from trees or gunning chainsaws or pretending to have lost a limb. My aunt, Donna Adams, worked tirelessly in the concession stand and basically everywhere she was needed. And my uncle Gerry was a constant presence who arguably loved that trail more than anyone. He was there every night of every year from start to finish, and although there are many stories about Gerry Adams and the Trail of Terror, my favorite is the one in which he shot a .357 into the air one afternoon when no one but he and Vince were around and somehow managed to shoot straight through a power line. Members of our family often remind Gerry that the things he did thirty years ago would get him arrested today. But despite the crazy stunts, Gerry managed to be loved by every kid who ever attended Powerplay or worked on the Trail of Terror.

There Is No East or West

Join hands then, brothers of the faith,
what e'er your race may be;
Who serves my Father as a son is surely kin to me[33]

During the early 1980s, as the church was experiencing tremendous growth in attendance, church leadership felt a call to expand its outreach, as directed in Acts 1:8, "to the uttermost parts of the earth." Colonial Hills Baptist, where Buford and Babs attended when they first moved to Atlanta, had been a strong advocate of foreign missions. Its main sanctuary had a beautiful map of the world painted on the front wall over the choir loft, and sparkling lights illuminated the spots on the map where the church's missionaries served. The new Missions ministry at Clayton Community was modeled somewhat after that of Colonial Hills, with a Missions committee and an annual conference. After the Missions committee was formed, the church called its first missionaries to the foreign field, a young couple named Gary and Donna Beach, who, incidentally, are still serving today in England.

---

33 Written by John Oxenham

As an example to members of the church's teaching on the tithe, Community Bible Church regularly committed twelve percent (a ten percent tithe plus an offering) of its income to missions. Mission conferences started as a weeklong event every February.[34] All missionaries – those who called the church home, and those supported by the church through gifts to various mission agencies – were invited back to the church to describe their ministries and to encourage people to give individually to their support. Buford says, "The Mission conference grew for a number of years to the point where we had probably twenty to thirty missionaries every year encouraging people to have a world view of ministry."

In 1980, Robert Rohm resigned his position as school principal so that he could attend Dallas Theological Seminary, and a search began for a new principal. Robert recommended a man named Kent Kelso to succeed him. Kent and his wife, Faye, had been missionaries with Christian Aviation Fellowship and had been instrumental in helping to build Jamaica Bible College in Mandeville, Jamaica.

But Buford and the Elders had misgivings about Kent solely because they didn't know him. Len McWilliams, a Georgia Tech graduate with a degree in management, had been an Elder for several years and had even served as chairman. Buford says, "I didn't really know Kent, and I tend to always look for someone with whom I have a history – someone I know – before I put them in a position with that much responsibility. We knew Len

---

34 Over the years, as the number of people willing to be at church every night of the week dwindled, they were shortened to Sunday through Wednesday.

McWilliams. He'd been a member of the church for a long time and was on the Board of Elders, so our choice was Len."[35]

Despite being passed over for the position as principal, Kent and Faye stayed in the church. They were devoted members, and Kent later served as Chairman of the Board of Elders. In late 1984, the Kelsos asked Babs and Buford to travel with them to Jamaica to visit the annual board meeting of a new ministry, a school for deaf children named Caribbean Christian Center for the Deaf. In January, the two couples boarded a plane in Atlanta bound for Montego Bay, Jamaica.

A *Los Angeles Times* article dated January 15, 1985, the same day they flew into Jamaica, began with this lead:

"KINGSTON, Jamaica — Riots touched off by sharp price increases for gasoline and propane gas paralyzed the country today, and demonstrators blocked roads and set fire to piles of tires. Police reported two dead."[36]

When their plane landed in Montego Bay, the Adams and Kelsos and about two dozen other people from ministries around the United States boarded a bus for the drive up the mountain to Mandeville. During that three-hour ride, the country erupted in riots over the price of gas. According to the same *Times* article, the government shut down, and businesses and schools were closed. Domestic flights were grounded.

------

35 Early in Len's tenure as principal, the school had about ten percent minority enrollment. He was walking down the halls of the school one morning, and he passed a class of kindergarten children lined up against the wall. As he walked by, a little African-American boy motioned for him. Len bent over the child and asked how he was doing. The little boy responded that he was fine but then said, "I know what's wrong with this place. There are too many white folks here."
36 http://articles.latimes.com/1985-01-15/news/mn-7328_1_riot-gas-prices

The group managed to get to the school in Mandeville without encountering any rioting, so they had no idea that the country was in turmoil. Buford says of the riots, "Six of us were going to stay at Jamaica Bible College down in Mandeville rather than at the deaf school. So we boarded the bus for the trip back into Mandeville, and we ran into about five hundred people who were rioting in the street. We were the only white people around. When they saw us on the bus, they began to shake their fists, and they began rocking the bus, pushing us back and forth. We were terrified, had no idea what would happen if they got on the bus. Thankfully, our driver, a Jamaican himself, was very cool. He put the bus in reverse and began to slowly back up, so that it didn't roll over anyone or hurt anyone. He managed to get us out of there, and we took an alternate route to the hotel.

The rioters overturned cars and burned them, then built barricades across roads to stop traffic. Buford and Babs and the people with them were trapped at the hotel. Unable to participate in the school's board meetings, they waited at their hotel in Mandeville for days while riots continued across the country. The day of their return flight to the States, Ernest Clark, a Jamaican landowner descended from a plantation family, showed up with his Land Rover, an old model with canvas sides. He delivered the group safely to the school, where they connected with a group of people who were riding back to the airport. Twelve people and their luggage were crammed into a Volkswagen van meant to hold eight or nine people.

Buford says, "We began the trip back to Montego Bay airport, sticking to back roads because the main roads had been rendered impassable by the rioting. We went through what's called the 'cockpit' part of the country, which is notorious for marijuana growing and other kind of illegal activities, and every few miles, we would run up on a barricade that had been constructed across the road – old tires, timbers, whatever they could find to block traffic. Another pastor and I were young and more athletic than most of the group, and so it became our job to ride shotgun and jump out when we came upon a barricade and quickly get enough cleared away so that the van could squeeze through, then jump back in before we got caught. All the way back, Bill and I threw tires. We could see people come out of their houses, running toward us with rocks in their hands, and we would get enough out of the way to let the van through, jump in, and take off. We did that all the way down the mountain to the airport. When we got to the airport, of course, it was in total chaos because all foreigners were trying to get out of the country. We managed, believe it or not, to get on an airplane that day. It was hours delayed, but we made it safely back to the United States. I don't think anyone on that van ever returned to Jamaica and the deaf school except for Babs and I and Kent and Faye. The fellow helping me toss tires out of the road was pastor of a church in Stone Mountain, Georgia, and he said to me that day, 'I'll never come back here again.'"

Over the years, Buford and Babs continued their travels to Jamaica. Kent and Buford served on the board of the Caribbean Christian Center for the Deaf, and during that time, the school built three campuses for deaf children in Jamaica with volunteer labor and contributions from many churches across the United States. Then, in the mid-1990s, there was an anti-American swell of sentiment that ran across the country, and the Jamaicans on the school's board politely asked the Americans to resign.

The church also sponsored several large one-time missions projects. One of those was funding the translation and publication of the New Testament into the language of a people known as the Guarani tribe.

In 1986, Robert DeNiro and Jeremy Irons starred in *The Mission*, a film about a group of eighteenth century Spanish Jesuits attempting to protect the Guarani, a remote South American tribe, from Portuguese slave traders after the Treaty of Madrid (1750) reapportioned a section of land in South America, making it a Portuguese colony. The forces of Portugal eventually descended upon the mission and slaughtered everyone. Only a very small group of the Guarani managed to escape into the jungle.

Today, the descendants of that tribe are very reclusive and, understandably, wary of outsiders. They make a living by producing handcrafts that they sell to other Indian tribes, who turn around and sell them to the white man. A professor of mathematics at the University of Texas, Robert Dooly, lived with the Guarani people for several years and translated their language into a written form. Using his work, Wycliffe Bible Translators published the New Testament in their language, and the church paid for that translation.

In 1987, Babs and Buford traveled to Iguazu Falls, a horseshoe-shaped waterfall near the border of Brazil and Argentina that is the largest in the world in terms of volume. There they presented copies of the translated New Testament to the Guarani tribal leaders and to every member of the tribe.

A trip to Indonesia a year later made Buford wonder if there might be a connection between foreign mission trips and national rebellions. He was invited to speak at a pastor's conference in Yogyakarta, a large city with a metro population of nearly 2.3

million people located on the same island as the capitol city of Jakarta.[37] The conference was to last a week, and it was for pastors who had been trained by Dr. Chris Marantika, a native of Indonesia who had graduated from Dallas Theological Seminary and gone home to start a seminary. Every year, three to four hundred Indonesians graduated from that seminary, then went to their native villages and established churches. More than half of these graduates were women. Students were required to have a church averaging at least thirty people in order to graduate from the seminary, even though establishing churches in Muslim villages meant risking their lives. Muslim activists would trap Christians in their church building on a Sunday morning, bar the doors, and set the church on fire. People were burned alive. Buford says, "They were often taken into the town square and beaten for daring to start a Christian church in a Muslim village, but that's the sort of bravery that was demonstrated by these folks. I felt unworthy to even be speaking to them."

He and Babs flew into Bali with Frank and Carlene Bailey, representatives from a mission agency called Partners International, and from there they flew to Yogyakarta. While they were there, the country erupted in revolution. General Suharto, a communist dictator who had ruled since 1966, was overthrown, and the country was in turmoil. The streets were dangerous, so Babs and Buford were basically locked in their hotel, a Holiday Inn owned by an English gentleman. Church leaders would drive to the hotel each day to pick them up and escort them to the campus of the seminary, where Buford would speak in the morning and in the evening.

When they arrived, the American dollar was worth around 12 Indonesian rupiah. By the time they left, it was worth around 80.

---

37 Commonly written and pronounced "Jogjakarta" or just "JOGH-jah"

"It worked out well for us because the four of us stayed an entire week at that hotel, ate all of our meals, including lobster every night, sent out our laundry, and the total bill for the four of us was, I believe, $157. As a matter of fact, we visited a bank during that time to get some cash, and people were using wheelbarrows to transport their rupiah from one part of the bank to another -- stacks three to four feet high of their currency because it was virtually worthless," Buford remembers.

Over the years, the church sponsored projects building churches and orphanages and schools in many countries. The church was deeply connected to Partners International and its representative, Frank Bailey, during the 1990s. The church supported a number of Partners International missionaries, and Bailey was continually offering the church a challenge to build a church here or an orphanage there.[38] When the projects were completed, he invited groups from the church to go see the finished products. Over the years, Buford and Babs visited China several times to dedicate churches built with donations from church members.

On their first visit to China, they arrived in Hong Kong after a fourteen-hour flight from Los Angeles and were immediately picked up by the local pastor chosen to serve as their escort. From there, they drove to Guangzhou, a city that served as their home base while they visited villages within a two-to-three hour drive from there.

"We would enter a small village, and if there were three hundred people living in that village, there would be three hundred people there to greet us, even in the middle of a weekday. They would set off firecrackers by the thousands to celebrate our arrival. We would be escorted into the church building that we had paid for and they had constructed, and they were generally small

---

38 Frank Bailey called these challenges "Missions: Possible."

buildings – maybe 35x70 feet, but very well constructed, pretty little buildings with a Chinese façade. I would speak, and then the local pastor who was escorting us would speak," Buford says.

When both men had finished their sermons, the Communist Minister of Religion and Culture for that particular region of China would stand and say a few words. In fact, a Minister of Religion and Culture was always one of the men escorting them through China. In China, there's a saying that "everything is true somewhere in China." And they also say, "It's a long way to Beijing," meaning the further you get from there, the less influence it has on local officials and local culture. In this particular part of communist China, Christianity was encouraged. During Buford and Babs' trip, officials would point out other villages and urge them to build churches in those places so that they could worship legally rather than in a home or in some underground facility, which was illegal. As long as the church had a building and was publicly recognized, Christian worship was allowed. The thing the Chinese government did not want was people to be meeting secretly because they could not be sure what was being taught.

On one occasion, they were way up in the mountains, in a small village hours away from civilization. After the long road trip, they needed a restroom. Using a mixture of sign language and slowly-spoken English, Babs asked a tiny lady from the village where she could find a restroom. The lady motioned for Babs to follow, and she led Babs out behind a barn and pointed to a little lean-to. Babs walked in, and there was a pit about six by six feet wide and four feet deep with a 2x10 lying across it. The trick was to walk out on the 2x10 and balance while going to the bathroom. If you failed to balance, God help you.

They were served the finest food each village had to offer on these visits. Buford says, "I remember on one occasion they served us bowls of pig entrail soup. My sense of smell is bad, so I had no problem with it, but Babs literally could not choke it down, so she would wait until the officials were not looking and pour her soup into my bowl."

On another occasion, they were served platters of boiled baby frogs. Thousands of them – each about the size of a finger-tip – were piled on a platter and served with a side of rice. Not eating what they served was an insult, so they braved all sorts of different foods over the years.[39] One host, who had attended seminary in the United States, leaned over to Babs one night during dinner, winked at her, and said, "You know, Americans are food starved. All you folks eat is chicken, beef, and pork. We eat everything."

In 2005, Mom and Dad traveled to China with several couples who had contributed to building churches through Partners International. Near the end of the trip, they spotted a restaurant advertising "American steaks" and decided they could use some good old American food.

I asked Mom to tell me the story of Dad's meltdown at a restaurant in China, fully intending to take notes and write it from those notes. But she brought me a couple of handwritten sheets of paper torn from a spiral notebook, and to be honest, I can't tell the story any better than she did. So here, in my mom's words, is the story of the Great China Steakhouse Incident:

Mission travels present numerous strange and wonderful challenges. One such trip to southern China in 2005 proved

---

39 They learned to travel with cans of tuna and packages of peanut butter crackers in their carryons.

to be quite trying. In Duan, we had trouble getting a decent night's rest on beds with no mattress – just plywood boards covered with a thin mat to lie on – the only way to sleep was on our backs with legs bent toward the ceiling.

The bathroom was so constructed that the shower was open on one side of the room with a drain on the other end, so that the floor stayed wet. A sign on the wall read, "Fall Carefully."

Needless to say, these conditions of sleep deprivation and stress seemed to addle us all, but Buford had had enough when we got to the city of Nanning and went to a restaurant claiming to have American food. We walked into the restaurant, and several Chinese men began trying to set up tables in a side room off the dining room for our large group. They ran tables this way and that numerous times, still not able to figure out adequate seating, until Buford exploded, yelling and waving his arms. He motioned for the men to move away and within just a few minutes had the tables in a suitable configuration, upon which he announced, "We don't need to worry about China taking over the free world when they can't even set up a few tables for lunch!"

I was cringing, imagining all sorts of retribution. It was Communist China, and I saw us not ever being able to leave. Our whole party stood around, mouths open, gawking in disbelief as he took control of the situation.

But he wasn't done. We ordered steaks, and they came out raw. Everyone, to a person, sent their steaks back, imagining all sorts of bad things happening from eating raw meat in that restaurant. Finally, Buford had had enough of people trying to get their steaks adequately cooked. He stood up from the table, marched into the kitchen, and the former grill man for the Dwarf House cooked our steaks for us.

I Am Loved at Community Bible Church

Have you ever seen the cartoon saying, "Please forgive me for the things I say when I'm hungry?" I'm sure an Adams inspired it. We're notorious for losing our minds when we've gone too long without food. Add no sleep to that, and it's a wonder the State Department isn't still trying to convince China to release a retired preacher from Florida.

This Is My Father's World

This is my Father's world
O let me ne'er forget
That though the wrong seems oft so strong
God is the ruler yet[40]

As the church continued to grow, new ministries and programs were added to meet the needs of the congregation. The senior citizen's ministry, called the Joy Club, began offering monthly outings and two or three trips every year for the church's over-fifty-five members. In response to a demonstrated need for professional Christian counseling services, a church member named Gary Lester, who was a licensed clinical social worker employed by the State of Georgia, came on staff in 1980 and opened the Clayton Counseling Center, which offered individual, family, marital, and premarital counseling. And with the expansion of cable television following the deregulation of the industry in 1984, new local channels were hungry for programming. The church formed a media ministry to tape and produce broadcasts of the Sunday morning services.

Still, two ministries weren't performing to Buford's satisfaction. They were the ones focused on teenagers – the youth ministry, now called Powerplay, and the Christian high school. Despite

---

40 Words by Maltbie D. Babcock

its success in attracting teens from Clayton County's public high schools, especially during the years Vince Pinyard had run it, countless other teens refused invitations to Powerplay based on the perception that it was "church." That the Youth Ranch and its successors would be swallowed up by the church was a problem Buford hadn't foreseen when the church started in 1970. Yet by the mid-1980s, it was apparent that the Reynolds Road property was Clayton Community Church, and the church just happened to have a youth ministry. Much of the early Youth Ranch's success, Buford and Jack had always believed, was due to the fact that it wasn't church. Teenagers didn't have to dress up in their Sunday best. Messages weren't delivered from an elevated pulpit, and to be sure, the music in no way resembled church music. Church leadership discussed the issue for a few years before deciding that the best solution would be to recreate something like the original Barton Drive Youth Ranch building on the property the church had purchased from Judge Reynolds's estate.

The new building was constructed in 1986 with mostly donated materials and volunteer labor. Mike Reid, a church member who owned a concrete company, donated the eighty-by-thirty-foot slab on which it was constructed, and on one summer day not long after the slab had been poured, the church held an old-fashioned barn raising. The new building had a large meeting room and an attached three-bedroom, two-bath apartment for the Powerplay director and his family.[41]

The Christian high school's issues were another matter. While the daycare, preschool, kindergarten, and elementary schools were all thriving, the high school was limping along with ten or fifteen students in each grade. Because of the expense of athletic

---

41 Jim Bennett, a teacher in the Christian school, had been hired to fill the vacancy left when Vince Pinyard resigned to pursue his studies.

programs, specialized teachers in high school classrooms, the costs for science labs, and other upper-level needs, the high school was losing money. It was increasingly difficult for the school to compete with what public high schools could offer their students. In addition, the Christian high school had often been viewed as a place where parents could send troubled teens in hopes of straightening them out. So the mix of students was approximately half who really wanted to be there and half angry at being yanked out of a public school and having to sit through Bible class every morning. After several years of debate, in 1988, Clayton Christian School discontinued grades nine through twelve.

People accused my father of waiting until his children no longer attended the high school to close it down, but that was probably a bit unfair. The truth is, he wanted all of us kids – my brother, Beau, my sister, Holly, and me -- in a public high school. I think the biggest reason was that he was afraid that teenagers who marinated too long in a sheltered Christian environment eventually began to view Christianity with a bit of disdain. Plus, he wanted us to prove that we did what was right when we weren't under the watchful eye of people who knew our parents. "It's easy to be a big fish in a small pond. Let's see what happens when you're a small fish in a big pond," was the way he put it.

Although I was in church every time the doors were open from the day the church started until I went off to college, I can only remember a handful of specific sermons, and of those, there are a couple of lines that will be with me forever. Dad used to say, "Good kids come out of good homes, and good kids come out of bad homes, but I've never seen a good kid come out of an inconsistent home." And this line, spoken when I was probably a sophomore in high school, put the fear of God in me: "One of these days, I'm going to stand in this pulpit and say, 'I told you so.' It'll be the day my three kids are grown, and I'm going to say, 'All the things on parenting I've taught over the years were right, and here are my three kids to prove it.'"

Growing up in the fishbowl of ministry, preacher's kids are subjected to intense scrutiny. Their father stands up on Sundays and basically tells hundreds, even thousands, of people how they should live their lives. Naturally, those people watch to make sure that what's good for the goose is good for the gander, and the pastor's entire family is under the microscope. Children feel the pressure and innately understand that it's unfair – after all, they didn't choose their father's profession – and they're too emotionally immature to be dealing with an impossible standard of perfection. So they must choose between two basic self-preserving strategies. Either they totally rebel and make a move designed to carve out a separate identity, which is the classic "naughty preacher's kid" people joke about. Or they become the perfect kids who never cross any line with so much as a big toe, careful protectors of the family image.

The rebel can cause some huge problems for the minister's family. In extreme cases, Dad could lose his job. More often, they just embarrass their parents, which is usually the intended effect of these angry kids.

The perfect kid, on the other hand, never feels quite good enough simply because perfection is perfectly impossible. For example, the first report card I took home in fifth grade had all As, and I was proud of it because I'd worked hard. My teacher took me aside as the bell was ringing to dismiss for the day and said to me, "This is great, but what you really need to work for now is straight A-plusses."

Remember the Scared Straight programs of the eighties and nineties? Based on the Academy Award-winning documentary called *Scared Straight!*, starring Peter Falk and Danny Glover, the programs took delinquent juveniles into the country's toughest prisons in order to rehabilitate them by showing them what they didn't want to become. All it took for me to be scared straight was my dad's words from the pulpit that Sunday. Deep down, I was terrified of doing something bad enough to cost my dad his job.

My brother and sister both graduated from Morrow Senior High School, but I loved Clayton Christian School, so Dad let me stay. I graduated in 1984 and went off to Bryan College, a small Christian liberal arts school in Dayton, Tennessee, where I was a small fish in a small pond. I was miserable away from home, so the next year, I transferred to Clayton Junior College (now Clayton State) and eventually earned a degree in English from Georgia State University.

I worked at the church throughout college. I had a small desk in the office of the church bookkeeper, Donna Glore. My job was to count the Sunday offering, prepare the church and school payrolls, and prepare every bank deposit for both the church and school – all under Donna's watchful eye, of course. Counting the offering every week meant that I had firsthand knowledge of who gave to the church and how much they gave.[42] Nearly thirty years later, I've never discussed that information with anyone, but I will say this: the lessons that stay with us forever are not so much the ones we hear with our ears. They're the ones we hear and then see demonstrated. Back then, I thought my Granddad Adams was a wealthy man. He and my uncle, Gerry, owned a vending

---

[42] I also learned that it was Gerry Adams who was wadding up cash into tiny balls just to give me headaches.

business, and I sometimes worked in their office helping count money and preparing bank deposits. I saw bags of coins coming in every day, like someone had found a sunken treasure ship. When I started counting the church offering, I saw that Granddad gave to the church generously, and I could have set my clock by his contributions because they were so regular. My grandparents never said the first word to me about giving, but they didn't have to. I'd seen the old wooden box Granddad had carved in the 1940s for their household expenses, the one with the category for their tithe, sitting on a shelf in their home office. At an impressionable age, I had a concrete example of someone who gave freely and prospered because of it. It helped me form an enduring belief that giving and receiving are two sides of the same coin.

The second lesson I learned -- and this was perhaps even more important for me as a teenager – was that my dad practiced what he preached. While he was encouraging church members to give, he was tithing regularly himself.

I'm not sure why, but any resentment I might have felt over being unfairly scrutinized as a preacher's kid didn't surface until I began to see it happen to my brother's kids years later and, to an extent, even my own children. When my daughter Morgan was in middle school, an unsuspecting teacher at the Christian school said to her something along the lines of, "You shouldn't be acting like the other kids because you're the preacher's granddaughter." I made a special trip to the school the next day and made it clear that no child should ever be held to a different standard because of whom his or her parents happen to be. As Christians, we are all to be about the business of becoming more like our Father in Heaven. Developing different standards for behavior, especially for children, is a way of making people feel either "better than" or "less than," and it is a violation of everything Jesus taught.

Trust and Obey

When we walk with the Lord
in the light of His Word
What a glory He sheds on our way!
While we do His good will,
He abides with us still,
And with all who will trust and obey[43]

By the mid 1980s, attendance at the Sunday morning services was larger than the church's 1,200-seat auditorium could hold. A second service was added at 8:30 a.m., with Sunday school for all ages meeting at 9:45, in between the 8:30 and 11:00 morning services. Eventually, a third service was added at 9:45, along with a second Sunday school session beginning at 11:00. Being out of space is always a good problem for a church to have, but Buford recognized it as a signal that the church would need to begin thinking about constructing a bigger auditorium. He calls it the "eighty percent rule," and it goes something like this: when a church service reaches eighty percent capacity on a regular basis, it will stop growing because people unconsciously feel too crowded. At that point, a church must either add another service or construct a new worship auditorium, or growth will come to a halt. And

---

43 Written by John H. Sammis

it is a universal truth that anything that isn't growing is dying. An interesting side note, Buford says, is that "you can have two services that are at forty to fifty percent capacity, and logic would tell you to combine them. But if you do that, you're in big trouble. You'll start to lose people."

All along, the church had planned eventually to construct a new sanctuary on the land purchased from the Reynolds estate. As they began discussing the new auditorium in earnest, a question arose: *Would it be better to build just a new worship center and somehow try to connect the two campuses, or should they attempt to sell the old campus and essentially start over on the twenty-nine acres up the road?* That question was partially answered when Buford contacted the pastor of the little Baptist church sitting on a few acres dividing Community's two parcels of land on Reynolds Road. Would they be willing to sell their property, he wondered. When the church turned down that request, he asked if Community might be able to purchase few feet of easement on the back of their property so that the church's two campuses might somehow be connected. They also said no to that offer.

In 1985, the church hired a consulting firm to study the ministry and to advise the staff and Elders on how to keep it growing. In a nutshell, the company came back with this recommendation: in order to thrive, you must get back to doing what you do well.[44] For Clayton Community Church, that had always been evangelism, and more specifically, using creative means to evangelize. Out of that, the church developed a new purpose statement: "To develop a dynamic church, through the grace and power of Christ, dedicated to the worship of God, to equipping the body for daily ministry, and to evangelizing the lost, both locally and beyond."

---

44 Otherwise known as "dance with the one that brung 'ya."

Trust and Obey

The Elders began tossing around ideas for how to fulfill the mandate from that purpose statement. In one of those discussions, Kent Kelso, who was Chairman of the Board, asked if the church had considered making another big move like it had when moving from Barton Drive to Reynolds Road. He pointed out that the church's membership seemed to be moving south, away from the urban sprawl of metro Atlanta. And the demographics of those visiting the church and joining as new members proved that it wouldn't be long before the majority of church members lived ten or fifteen miles down Interstate 75 in Henry County. Buford says, "I remember thinking that people would be willing to drive ten or fifteen miles one day a week, on Sundays, for church. But I didn't believe that they would be willing to make that drive every day of the week to bring their children to school and then to come to church on Sundays."

The Elders began looking at other churches around the country for ideas and found one that had successfully planted a "daughter" church, Briarwood Presbyterian in Birmingham, Alabama. In their search, they also found a church in South Carolina that had successfully developed retirement communities on church property. They began exploring the possibility of doing something similar on the acreage purchased from Judges Reynolds and Foster.

At the same time, the church began exploring the possibility of building a second location in Henry County. In 1986, a developer from Florida named J. T. Williams purchased approximately twenty-five hundred acres off of Hudson Bridge Road in Stockbridge for the purpose of developing a mixed-use golf community. The church saw this as an answer from the Lord, an opportunity to reach the thousands of new families that would eventually move into that area. In July of 1987, the church published a brochure titled "Mission: Project Judea" to explain the concept of establishing a daughter church in Henry County. Along with the brochure was a survey for members with questions like *How do you feel about our congregation worshipping in two places? How do you think we should fulfill our purpose as a church to evangelize the lost? Do you think spending money to build at a new location in Henry County is a wise investment of our outreach funds? Would you financially support a building program for a new location in Henry County?*

In response to that survey and as part of the new purpose of "equipping the saints," Clayton Community sponsored a church growth seminar by Win Arn, co-author of the book *How to Grow Your Church: Conversations About Church Growth.* Promotional posters encouraging church members to "envision our church exploding with more life and vitality . . . reaching out and winning more people . . . and expanding our horizons" featured a full-length picture of my dad with his left hand outstretched and his right index finger pointing toward the sky. While perusing old church files, I came across the original black and white photo of him shot for this poster. Dad didn't remember the picture, so I sent it to my brother asking if he knew what the picture had been used for.

He circulated the picture to the church staff, but none of them could remember it. So they created a contest to see who could come up with the best caption for the photo. The winning caption: "UP YOUR TITHES."

My mother later found a copy of the promotional poster. Apparently, it was supposed to be a sort-of Uncle Sam "I Want

You" idea, telling members he wanted them to attend the seminar, except Dad was pointing into the air rather than right at the audience. Thirty years later, the tithing caption seems to me to be a better fit.

I mentioned earlier that we lived on five acres in a community made up of church and family members. It was in Ellenwood, very close to the Clayton and Henry County lines, and I don't think my parents ever imagined themselves moving from there when they built the place.

We were pretty self-sufficient on Hebron Way. Of course, Dad had the epic garden with its twenty-three varieties of squash. We ate meat and eggs from my grandfather's farm. Dad had also planted grape vines and nearly one hundred fruit trees on that land. And for a brief period of time, he dabbled in beekeeping.

Don and Terri McGinnis, longtime members of the church, lived on several acres that backed up to our place. Don called my dad one day and said, "Buford, would you like to go in with me to buy a couple of beehives?" Dad jumped on the offer.

Don found a man who had some beehives for sale. The man wanted $100 for his three hives, and he offered to throw in a beekeeper's hat with the hives. Don and Dad drove to his house and picked up the hives. They set them out in the woods between their two houses. All summer long, the bees worked hard producing honey.

That fall, when it came time to rob the hives, Don and Dad met in the woods. Don had wisely purchased a new beekeeper's suit that covered every part of his body. But Dad just put on a long-sleeved shirt, a pair of overalls, and that old used beekeeper's hat.

They approached the first hive, lifted the lid, pulled out the slats, and stole the honey. The docile bees gave them no trouble.

Taking the honey from the second hive was, like the first, as easy as pulling a jar of the stuff off of a grocery store shelf. But when they got to the third hive and lifted its lid, they saw that the bees were stirred up.

Dad remembers the scene: "There's an old saying about angry queens producing angry hives, and this queen must have livid because the minute we opened that lid, those bees started swarming us. We still didn't think we had a problem. A few of them got to me on my hands, but they couldn't sting through my clothing, so I was okay."

About that time, my brother's English springer spaniel, Champ, showed up to see what they were doing. The bees swarmed him, and the poor dog took off through the woods, yelping and crying. It must have tickled some sort of sadistic streak in Dad because he doubled over laughing at Champ's misery.

He stopped laughing, though, when he detected some movement inside the screen of his old beekeeper's hat. Looking down toward his nose, he realized that a lone bee had somehow managed to penetrate the fortress of that hat. When the bee landed on the tip of his nose, Dad panicked. He made a monumental mistake by yanking off the hat. Instantly, the swarm descended upon his head, and he took off through the woods, yelping and crying.

"I don't know how many stings I got, but I made it home, and I remember lying on our living room floor moaning. Babs was giving me Benadryl, and the kids kept coming in, laughing, and calling me 'Elephant Man.'"

Dad's beekeeping days were over. He called Don McGinnis and told him he could have the bees, the hives, the honey, and especially the old beekeeper's hat, which was probably still lying on the ground next to the hives.

Sadly, their days at Hebron Way were also numbered. Several trucking firms secured zoning for huge warehouses very near the property. Afraid that it would affect their property values, the families in our neighborhood gradually began moving out, and like most of the people moving out of Clayton County at the time, they relocated in Henry County.

Blessed Assurance

I in my Savior am happy and blest;
Watching and waiting, looking above,
Filled with His goodness, lost in his love[45]

Buford was always hesitant to preach about giving. He hated asking people for money, but in a ministry dependent upon the financial contributions of its members, it was a necessity. Every October, staff members submitted their estimates of their ministry's needs for the upcoming year. Buford took those numbers, plus estimated operating expenses for the church grounds, printing and postage, staff salaries, and every other line item in the budget, and used them to put together a proposed budget for the new year. The church's finance committee took those numbers and, with a few minor changes here and there, approved the proposal. That yearly budget was printed, usually in a version condensed to show the main operating categories – Missions, Building Operations, Debt Retirement and Operating Contingency, Ministries, Personnel, Support Services, and Office and Vehicle Expenses -- with emphasis on what the church's weekly offering needs would be. In mid-November, that budget

---

45 Written by Fanny Crosby

was presented to the congregation, and members were asked to fill out a "commitment card" indicating what they intended to give over the course of the next year.

During the 1970s and 80s, the church held a yearly Stewardship Banquet much like the fundraising banquets of the early Youth Ranch years. The Stewardship Banquet, free to members, offered a catered dinner, special music, testimonies from members about what tithing meant to them, and then a brief message from Buford in which he urged every family to turn in a commitment card. A common challenge he presented came from a verse in the last book of the Old Testament: "'Bring the whole tithe into the storehouse, that there may be food in my house. Test me in this,' says the Lord Almighty, 'and see if I will not throw open the floodgates of heaven and pour out so much blessing that you will not have room enough to receive it'" (Malachi 3:10, NIV). The challenge, of course, was to commit to a tithe and see if God was as good as this promise. After the banquet, the finance committee would meet, and the final budget would be adjusted to reflect the church's projected contributions for the upcoming year.

Over the years, many of the church's building campaigns were launched in a similar manner – a fundraising banquet during which the need was presented, followed by an opportunity to pledge financial support. And every time Buford asked church members to give, he made this promise: "Your pledge card is between you and God, and no one but the church's finance committee will see it, and that is only to assess what our giving will be in the next year. We will never contact you if you are unable to meet your commitment, and we promise that if you ever come to the conclusion that you have not been blessed because you've given, you can call us, and we will refund every cent."

In the fifty-year history of the ministry, the church has only been asked one time for a refund.

In addition to financial contributions, the church has received some interesting gifts over the years. A lady once offered to deed a piece of property to the church -- an acre in a bad part of Atlanta. Buford drove over to look at it, but it was overgrown, and he couldn't see much of it from the road. The church accepted her gift with the intention of putting it on the market. After a few months, they received a letter from the City of Atlanta stating that they must either tear down the house that was on the property or rehabilitate it, and that they must secure it so that no one could enter. Buford took a couple of men with him to investigate, and sure enough, there was a house on the lot -- a decrepit, windowless structure. To their surprise, people were living in it. Upon investigation, they learned that an enterprising gentleman had rented it out to approximately twenty homeless people. The church, in essence, owned a crack house and was responsible for the expense of tearing it down. After evicting all the "tenants," they found a way to secure it, and to her credit, the lady who gave them the property took it back.

On another occasion, a man in the church donated three lots in a gated golf course community in San Jose, Costa Rica. The church had no interest in keeping those properties, so Buford found an English-speaking real estate agent in Costa Rica, a man named Pablo, who listed the lots. It took nearly a year, but Pablo finally secured contracts on all three. The buyers were businessmen from Colombia who wanted to move their families to Costa Rica for safety reasons.

Buford flew to Costa Rica for the closings. It was 2000, a few years before the country became the hot tourist destination it is now, and at that time, there were no computers or even typewriters used to record real estate transactions. Everything was recorded by hand. In addition, to avoid heavier taxation, every transaction had to be listed as a corporate transaction with corporate books, including a minutes book and a financial ledger. Buford carried with him nine books, three for each corporation, on the flight to San Jose.

They held all three closings on the same day, and at each closing, Buford received a cashier's check from a bank. However, no bank in Costa Rica accepted cashier's checks, even from another bank. So he had to go to the bank issuing each cashier's check and cash it into $100 bills. Because of the crime rate in that city, each bank had scanners and guards – one inside the bank and one outside – armed with Uzis. Three different times that day, he emptied his pockets, passed by a scanner, then went into a bank and cashed a $35,000 check. He stuffed the cash into his computer bag, and at 4:30 that afternoon, he and Pablo rushed to the Pan American bank with $105,000 in cash that needed to be converted to a letter of credit because he obviously couldn't enter the United States with that much cash. As they were driving through downtown San Jose with a bag crammed full of hundred dollar bills, rushing to get to the bank before it closed, Buford said, "Pablo, this is crazy!"

Pablo grinned and said, "Don't worry. This is all part of the adventure!"

In the early 1980s, a gentleman who owned several "buy-here, pay-here" auto lots around the city of Atlanta began attending church regularly. Every Christmas, he stopped by the church to bring money and toys for the church to give to underprivileged children, but he was shy and reticent and never quite seemed to make eye contact with anyone. As he exited church one day, however, he told Buford that if he ever needed a good deal on a used car to call him.

I Am Loved at Community Bible Church

"When my oldest daughter turned sixteen, I called him and said, 'I need a car for my daughter,' and he said, 'Okay, I'll work on that,'" Buford remembers. "A few days later, I walked into my office, and my assistant said, 'There was a man here who left these keys. He said there's a little green Chevette in the parking lot and to try it out to see if you like it.' I walked outside, and sure enough, there was a cute little Chevy Chevette sitting there. I called him later and said, 'My daughter's driven the car and likes it. What do I owe you?' He said, 'Nothing. I'm giving it to you.' I told him I couldn't take the car, but he insisted."

Two years later, he did the same thing when Beau turned sixteen. Another car appeared in the church parking lot, and he wouldn't take a penny for it, either. He's still in the church today, and he still has a soft heart when it comes to children, the church, and his pastor.

Dad misspoke a bit when he told that man I liked the car. The truth is, I loved it. When I turned sixteen, even though I'd had summer jobs for several years, I didn't have the money to buy myself a car. And my parents certainly couldn't afford to buy me one. So when I got out of school one day and Dad walked me out to the parking lot and handed me the keys to a 1976 sea foam green Chevy Chevette, I was the happiest girl on the planet.

The 1976 Chevy Chevette ultimately made *Time* Magazine's list of worst cars ever made. But mine was a champ. That car got me around Clayton County during my junior and senior years of high school, and it carried me safely to and from Bryan College, north of Chattanooga, Tennessee, throughout my freshman year of college. It had a few quirks – the windshield wipers sometimes didn't work, so I had to pull off the road in heavy rain; the blinker switch broke off the steering wheel, which meant I had to hold it in my hand and stick it in the hole to turn on my blinkers; and I couldn't park on hills because sometimes the transmission was ornery and wouldn't let me put the car in park (I'd just leave it in drive and pull the emergency brake hard on those occasions). But it did have a stellar cassette tape deck, and I can still hear Andre Crouch, who was the opening act for Santana in the late 1970s and the first contemporary Christian artist to appear on *Saturday Night Live* and the *Tonight Show with Johnny Carson*, belting out "I Don't Know Why" as I drove my brother and sister to school every morning. That car goes down in history as the nicest thing someone I've never even met did for me.

Horace Adams on a ship bound for the Philippines during World War II.

Horace, Glennis, Buford, and Gerry Adams, early 1950s.

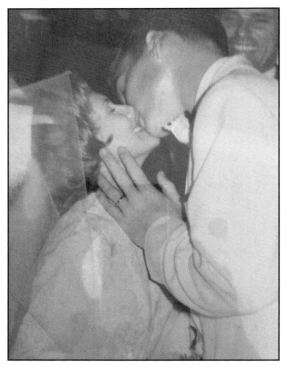

Buford and Babs' wedding, August 30, 1963.

Babs and Buford (2nd and 3rd from right) with a group of campers bound for Boca Raton, Florida.

Buford speaking at an early Youth Ranch meeting, circa 1966.

The first Atlanta Youth Ranch building, late 1960s.

The entrance to the first Atlanta Youth Ranch.

Bob Kohl, who wrote the church's articles of incorporation, with his wife, Carol, and daughter Dottie in front of the Youth Ranch building before one of the first church services. Buford Adams looks on. Jack Bartlett in background between the Kohls. Circa December 1970.

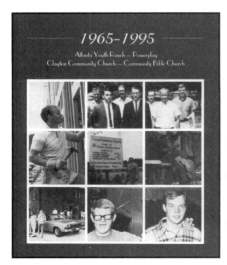

The cover of the ministry's 30th Anniversary program. Clockwise from top left: Buford helping frame the Reynolds Road Youth Ranch building, the Youth Ranch's first Board of Directors, Buford speaking in the first Youth Ranch meeting room, Buford and Johnny Raulins, the entrance to the first Youth Ranch meeting room (located on the back side of the Ranch building)

Preparing the new Reynolds Road auditorium for its first service, Easter Sunday 1973.

Crowd gathering for Sunday morning service, circa 1973.

Buford in front of the Reynolds Road property, circa 1975.

Clayton Christian School Christmas pageant, circa 1975.

Ticket to the ill-fated "God Bless America" Bicentennial celebration. The disclaimer at the bottom reads, "In event of overflow crowds, seats cannot be guaranteed."

Front side of a "Round Tuit." The backside reads, "I'll come to church when I get 'A-Round Tuit.'"

The "main" building at 5900 Reynolds Road, circa mid-1980s.

An aerial shot of 5900 Reynolds Road, circa mid-80s.

The auditorium at 5900 Reynolds Road, circa mid-80s.

*Buford in his office on
Reynolds Road, mid-80s.*

*Full-body shot of Buford taken for
a promotional poster, late 1980s.*

*Left to right: Jim Rinehart,
Buford Adams, James
Matthews, and Kent Kelso
at the Caribbean Christian
Center for the Deaf during
its annual board meeting,
circa early 1990s.*

Horace and Glennis Adams, late 1990s.

Beau, Kim, Madison, and Chase
Adams after Beau received his PhD in
Organizational Leadership, June 2012.

The Adams family at Buford and Babs' 50th Wedding Anniversary, August 30, 2014. Bottom row, from left: Alice Weber (Babs' mother), Horace Adams, Joe Phillips, Babs. 2nd row, from left: Hunter Hutcheson, Kate Phillips, Faith Phillips, Grace Phillips, Buford. 3rd row, from left: Sandi Adams Hutcheson, Lauren Hutcheson, Holly Adams Phillips, Beau Adams, Kim Adams. Top row: Morgan Hutcheson. Not pictured: Chase and Madison Adams.

*Debbie and Toney Jones with Jack Bartlett
at the Adams's 50th Anniversary*

Morgan, Lauren, and Hunter Hutcheson with the traveling portrait of their grandfather at Buford and Babs' 50th Anniversary.

Beau Adams speaking to a new members' class, 2014

Beau baptizing Adrianna Worley in the portable baptistry set up in the church atrium, 2014.

A selfie of Beau and children in Kodaikanal, India, during a June 2014 mission trip.

The Jodeco Road location as it looks today.

More About Jesus

More about Jesus, let me learn[46]

Truett Cathy, the founder of Chick-Fil-A and Buford's first boss, was another friend of the ministry over the years. When the Youth Ranch first opened, he donated the money to purchase sound equipment. And every month for many years, the church received a small monthly contribution from Chick-Fil-A.

Truett taught a fifth-grade boys' Sunday school class at the Baptist church where he was a member. One Sunday during the early days of the Youth Ranch, he invited Buford and Babs to visit his church, and he had Buford teach the Sunday school class for him. After church, they went to his home for lunch. The home was situated on about 160 acres on the Flint River in Lovejoy. Buford tells this story about that day: "After lunch, we walked out to his stable where he kept a number of horses. He asked us if we wanted to ride, and we told him yes. He gave Babs a nice, calm little horse, and he said, 'Buford, I think you're able to handle a more spirited horse.' I don't think I'd ever ridden a horse in my life, but I didn't want to disappoint Truett Cathy, so I said, 'Sure.' He put me on a horse, and as soon as he let go of the reins, that horse took off running as fast as he could. Babs still laughs about it today, saying she could hear me yelling, 'Whoa! Whoa!

---

46 Words by Eliza E. Hewitt

Whoa!' I was terrified. I couldn't get the horse to stop, and as he ran under a tree to try to knock me off, I leaned forward and hugged his neck. I survived that, but then the horse started running full gallop toward a fence. I thought he was going to jump the fence, and I had no idea how to take a jump. I simply jumped off the horse at a full gallop."

Buford and Truett remained friends throughout the years, and Buford says the older man often said to him, "Buford, everyone thinks they can run a restaurant and a church. But it's not true."

Nearly thirty years after they met, another invitation from Truett Cathy would change Buford's life. Chick-Fil-A had recently moved their headquarters to a beautiful new building on several wooded acres off of Buffington Road in College Park, not far from the Atlanta airport. Cathy invited Buford to deliver the morning devotional at a weekly Chick-Fil-A staff meeting.

After the staff meeting, a company executive complimented Buford on the message and then asked, "Where did you go to seminary?"

"I had to answer that I hadn't gone to seminary," Buford remembers. "I graduated from Mercer University with a degree in psychology, but I never went to seminary.[47] And it kind of embarrassed me. I started to think, you know, I'm the pastor of a pretty good-sized church, and I really should have some seminary training."

He began to research seminaries, but his options were limited. It was 1986, long before low-residency and online college degrees were widely available. But New Orleans Baptist Theological Seminary had recently opened a satellite campus in Atlanta. Students took two four-hour classes every Monday throughout

---

47 After moving to Atlanta in 1965 to start the Youth Ranch, Buford enrolled at Mercer, where he completed his undergraduate degree in 1971.

the year and attended three week-long residencies in New Orleans each year. Buford enrolled, and in 1990, he received his Master of Divinity degree.

"Then I decided that, having gone to college for five years and seminary for four, I might as well finish the job. I checked around to find which seminaries wouldn't require me to take Greek or Hebrew because I'm not all that great at languages," Buford says. The answer was practically in his backyard. Columbia Theological Seminary, an old-line, well-respected school in Decatur, was in partnership with Union Theological Seminary, one of the most prestigious in the country, and they offered a Doctor of Ministry program that operated on the low-residency premise (long once-a-week sessions versus daily classes) and didn't require Greek or Hebrew. He earned his doctorate from Columbia in 1993.[48]

"It changed me, I think, for the better," Buford says. "I was a lot more of an ideologue before I went to seminary. I thought I had all the answers. It also opened my eyes to accepting people who had different theological views, to realizing they had a pretty good case for their views, just like I had a pretty good case for mine. I learned that we can disagree and still get along."

That weekly drive into Decatur did something else. On his way to Columbia for classes, Buford drove past empty strip malls and, worse yet, abandoned churches with trees growing through cracks in the aged asphalt. He began to worry about what would happen if Clayton County became a rundown area of metro Atlanta like Decatur had become, and that made him nervous about what the future held for the Reynolds Road location.

---

48 Jack Bartlett followed in his footsteps, graduating from New Orleans Seminary in 1993, and earning a Doctor of Ministry degree from Columbia International University (Columbia, South Carolina), in 2002.

I Am Loved at Community Bible Church

If you ask my children what are some of their mother's favorite sayings, they'll most likely come back with, "The most important thing you get from an education is learning what you don't know."

Education is a valued commodity in our family, and I credit my parents for that.

Dad's decision to pursue his master's and doctoral degrees profoundly affected our whole family. In 1987, for example, my mother went back to school, graduating from Georgia State University in 1990 with a Bachelor of Fine Arts degree in Illustration. Her college carpool buddy was my brother, who graduated from Georgia State in 1991 with a B.A. in Communications. Having that many family members in college often led Dad to joke that he was suffering from "maltuition."

Beau would later earn the same Master of Divinity degree from New Orleans Baptist Seminary that Dad holds and then go on to earn a PhD in Organizational Leadership. My little sister, Holly, holds two master's degrees and is finishing her PhD in Cognitive Psychology. I began working on a master's degree in Journalism at Georgia State in 1989. I didn't get too terribly far into it before I got pregnant with my first child and dropped out, but I was determined that I would one day continue my education. In 2010, I finally claimed title to a MFA in English, and because I simply could not be outdone by the other members of my family, I finished a PhD in Creative Writing in 2014.

Sadly, throughout history, organized religion has had a tenuous relationship with education. A good example of that is the Bible itself.

Johannes Gutenberg invented the printing press in 1436, and both *The Biography Channel* and *A&E* have named Gutenberg as the single most influential person of the second millennium, ahead of Shakespeare, Galileo, and Columbus.

Here's why: the printing press meant that several identical editions of the same book could be printed in a relatively short time, while it probably would have taken a scribe at least a year to hand write one copy of the Bible. Gutenberg's invention led to more and more printing shops springing up all over Europe, and people began to realize they could make money off of books. Soon, printers were trying to guess how many copies a particular book could sell, and books turned into a speculative business. By 1500, books were a profitable endeavor, and there may have been as many as ten to twelve million books in Europe.

The desire for knowledge among the growing middle class combined with the availability of classical texts from ancient Greece and Rome to help fuel the Renaissance. In other words, books can be partially credited for taking humanity out of the Dark Ages. For the first time in history, texts could be widely dispersed. As a result, political, intellectual, scientific, religious, and cultural ideas spread rapidly.

As the Renaissance progressed, literacy rates rose. And the mass production of books made more information available to the masses. However, this spread of information was met with great resistance. The Roman Catholic Church, the dominant institution of medieval Europe, realized that because people could read, they had access to other views on the meaning of certain Scriptures. In 1487, Pope Innocent VIII mandated that all books be pre-screened by church authorities before copies were allowed to be printed.

The church also banned versions of the Bible printed in any language other than Latin—a language that few lay people understood. Church leaders feared Bibles translated into local vernacular because the more people who could read the Scriptures for themselves, the less control the church had over how the Bible was interpreted. And that made it very hard to control people.

Allowing religion to dictate who is educated and what can be taught is disastrous to a culture. I think of the bestselling *Reading Lolita in Tehran: A Memoir in Books*, the story of an Iranian college professor, Azar Nafisi, who secretly taught Western classics to a group of seven young women in Tehran during the mid-1990s, at a time when fundamentalists controlled the universities and Islamic morality squads were raiding homes. Nafisi writes, "Evil . . . lies in the inability to 'see' others, hence to empathize with them. . . . We are all capable of becoming the blind censor, of imposing our visions and desires on others" (315). The antidote to this fundamentalism is education because it teaches us that others' opinions are just as valid as our own, something my father discovered during his time at Columbia.

Isn't that, after all, the message of Jesus Christ? He didn't come to Earth to throw His weight around as God's Son by imposing a set of rules and then smacking people for not keeping those rules. He came as an example of how God wants us to act, and in doing so, showed tremendous empathy for every person who crossed His path. As a twelve-year-old boy, Jesus went missing. Mary and Joseph found him in the temple, " . . . sitting among the teachers, listening to them and asking them questions" (Luke 2:46, NIV). He was thirsty for education.

I was incredibly lucky to grow up in a family that valued education, and the church has been the better, I believe, for having had leadership who have felt God's call to pursue higher learning.

I can only think of a handful of things that, once they're yours, can never be taken away by another person. An education is one, and a personal relationship with God is another.

Deep and Wide

Deep and wide, deep and wide
There's a fountain flowing deep and wide[49]

By the fall of 1987, church leadership had to make a decision on how and where the church would expand. The majority of the church's membership supported the idea of building a daughter church in Henry County, yet it seemed cheaper (and easier) to move that half-mile up Reynolds Road to the property the church already owned.

Buford and most of the Elders were, by that time, convinced that the opportunity for greater growth and ministry lay in building a second campus in Henry County. They decided to proceed with the plan to open a second location in Henry County and to build a new educational building on the adjacent Reynolds Road property while seriously studying the idea of developing a retirement community on the remaining acreage.

They asked a local real estate agent to help them find twelve to twenty reasonably priced acres in a central Henry County location. But it was James McGuire, an Elder and longtime member, who suggested they inquire about a kudzu-covered, triangle-shaped piece of property on Jodeco Road less than a mile from Interstate 75.

---

49 Words and music by Sidney Cox

The property was purchased in late 1987, and preliminary sketches were drawn for a master building plan on that site in addition to one for the new educational building on Reynolds Road, which would house part of the Christian school on weekdays and a portion of Sunday school on Sunday mornings.

For the first time in the history of the ministry, the church decided to hire outside help for a fundraising campaign. Church Membership Services, Inc., evaluated the financial structure of the church and studied the giving potential of its membership before providing a detailed plan for a campaign that included training materials for the church staff and campaign volunteers plus all of the campaign's printed materials. The fundraising campaign was named "Partners in Progress: Dare to Dream," and it was launched on March 27, 1988, the day designated as Victory Sunday.

The large Partners in Progress brochure gave a brief history of the ministry, starting with the Youth Ranch's inception in 1965. The history ended with these words: "During the past seventeen years, the Lord has blessed us beyond our wildest imagination. When 35 of us gathered in a half-finished Youth Ranch building surrounded by swamp land and power line easement, we could scarcely have dreamed of 75,000 square feet of buildings, forty acres of prime real estate, a vibrant congregation of 1,800, and a mission outreach literally around the world. Yet that dream is being played out before us today." It went on to ask readers to imagine a new educational facility at the corner of Reynolds and Huie Roads, estimating that forty to forty-five percent of campaign funds would be used for that facility.

Then it moved to the Henry County portion of the project. "Beautiful property just a stone's throw from Interstate 75 on Jodeco-Flippen Road is the location for our second worship center. This area is literally exploding with homes and promises to be the fastest residential area in all of Georgia in the next few years."[50]

The congregation's response to the campaign was better than the church staff and Board of Elders could have imagined, and the church began making plans for expansion in both Clayton and Henry Counties.

In a memo to Buford dated December 12, 1989, Charles Swift presented the results of a vote by the Board of Elders based upon the feasibility study he had conducted in September and October of that year regarding the development of a retirement community on the Reynolds Road property. The study had been extensive, and the numbers provided by Gene Barber Homes, Inc., in Fayetteville, Georgia, validated his findings. According to Swift's memo, the Elders voted unanimously to abandon that idea because

> the cost per acre ratio was too high to support the level of town house we considered, the 'up front' development cost to build such a facility would exceed $500,000 (for streets, sewers, water, curb and gutter, landscaping, etc., not buildings), and it ceased to become a ministry and would become a development, which would put the church in a position of becoming a "commercial developer"; we did not feel this was wise.

The memo goes on to say that the ball fields that the church had built on the property had never been accessible from the 5900 Reynolds Road buildings and therefore had never been used as intended. In addition, a vacant lot fronting Highway 54 that had been used as parking for the Trail of Terror had just been sold to

---

[50] Little did church leaders (or anyone else, for that matter) know that Henry County would consistently make the list of America's top ten fastest growing counties in the early 2000s, with a population that between 2000 and 2010 went from 119,514 to 203,922 (source: CensusViewer.com).

a developer planning to build a shopping center. The sale meant the Trail would lose its parking lot. The memo concludes with these words:

> In view of all this and the rising cost of property tax in Clayton County, the Board of Elders believes we should market the property [on which the ball fields are situated]. This was a unanimous decision of the Board. In less than two weeks, we received a contract from the developer of the neighboring property.

Although the retirement community idea was abandoned, the plan to construct additional educational space on the property remained intact.

The study also recommend proceeding with the plans for the Jodeco Road property, so in May 1990, the church hired a Stockbridge architect named Darrel Rutherford to design a master plan for that spot. Construction began in 1991 on the first phase of that plan, a building that would house a 1,000-seat sanctuary, approximately twenty rooms that could be used as offices, nursery or Sunday school space, and, for the first time in the history of the church, an architectural detail that would seal its identity as a church – a steeple.

That first construction project at the Jodeco Road address was complicated. The twenty kudzu-covered acres needed extensive grading and infrastructure preparation. Unlike the handshake agreements with Gus Haynie that began the ministry's first four building projects, hiring a builder for this one involved a bidding process and a signed contract. Darrel Rutherford, the architect, oversaw the process, and during construction, he became quite frustrated because he believed the builder wasn't following his direction. He threatened to resign from the project. "I had to go to bat for the architect," Buford says. "I remember calling up the head of the company and having him meet me on site and explaining to him that he was either going to follow the terms of the contract and listen to our architect and do as the architect suggested or I was going to take legal action. At that particular time, we were in a recession, and there was very little building going on. So they did follow the architect's direction, and the building was finished beautifully. It was finished on time and on budget, but as a result of constructing that building for us, the builder went bankrupt. I think our building probably cost him a couple of hundred thousand dollars more than we actually paid for it."

In preparation for the opening of the Jodeco Road location, the church began a massive promotional campaign, both internally and externally. Members were surveyed to find out which location they planned to attend. Then they were asked to volunteer for a telephone canvass called "The Phone's For You." Jack Bartlett chuckles at the memory of watching Hugh McDonald and some of his co-workers from BellSouth install five new phone lines and a bank of thirty phones at the Reynolds Road location for the two-week phone-a-thon. Volunteers sat in the school cafeteria every evening dialing furiously and inviting those who answered to church. The script for those phone calls is long gone, but each of the 25,000 people called during that campaign heard about the new facility opening in the fall of 1992 on Jodeco Road in Stockbridge. Hugh says, "I know that in this day and time we wouldn't last one night before they closed us down!"

A brochure with an invitation to opening day was mailed to every household in Henry County. Its caption was "The New Kid on the Block Has Been Around the Block." While an obvious allusion to the New Kids on the Block, a boy band that was enormously popular in the late eighties and early nineties, the point of the brochure was that although a new church was opening, it was an established institution with a rich history in a neighboring community.

In church one Sunday morning, of the choir members, Dannie Chastain, sang a hilarious rendition of Garth Brooks' "Friends in Low Places."

"Both Places"
Words By Dannie Chastain
Sung to the tune of Garth Brooks' "I've Got Friends In Low Places"

A few years ago,
The Lord said "Ya know
You outta build yourselves another church"
So we decided to build
In a kudzu field,
Sometimes I wonder if we'd done our research
Well I didn't know
Which way I should go
I'd been there for such a long time
I was singing the blues
My friends were splitting in two
The Lord said "Boy, don't you whine!"

(Chorus)
Cause I got friends in Both Places,
Where the preaching's strong
And the music chases my blues away
Now I'll be ok
I can't wait to see your smiling faces
'Cause this church right here is like an oasis
So I got friends in both places

Now Buford still swears
He's gonna preach there
And here on that same day
He says, "I'll get in my car
It's not really that far
I won't let nothing get in my way"
Now to make it each week
I'm sure he'll speak
To a few Police Officers,
One more traffic fine
We'll have to drop a few dimes
And buy him a helicopter!

Deep and Wide

The church on Jodeco Road opened its doors November 8, 1992. That day, approximately five hundred people worshipped at the Reynolds Road property in Clayton County, which was dubbed the "North campus," and eight hundred people, about forty percent church members and sixty percent newcomers, attended the "South campus" on Jodeco Road. A commemorative plaque on the side of that first building notes the names of those who served on the building and finance committees for the new location. Three of those men, Bill Barton, Rod Suarez, and Ben Lopez, were around in the early years of the Youth Ranch and church – in fact, Barton was an original Youth Ranch board member, and Lopez was one of the founding members of the church. In addition, familiar names were inscribed on the pews in that new building -- Horace and Glennis Adams and Charles and Arnette Swift, the Youth Ranch's first donors, gave generously to the construction of the ministry's newest building.

Because the church was now located in both Henry and Clayton Counties, the name "Clayton Community Church" no longer fit,[51] so that same year, the ministry began operating under the name Community Bible Church, and the school changed its name to Community Christian School.

Buford had been preaching multiple services for several years, and that didn't change with the opening of the new South campus. For the next four years, he would preach an early service at 8:00 a.m. in Clayton County, then drive south to speak at 9:30, and finish with an 11:00 service in Clayton County. Steve Shivers

---

[51] This also did away with the "Satan Community" moniker. The decline of the Independent Baptist Church movement about this time plus the fact that many churches had succumbed to temptation and were now hosting their own Easter Sunday egg hunts most likely saved the church from another one.

also commuted between the two churches, leading the choir and orchestra and the congregational singing for those services. Jack Bartlett did their commute in reverse, so that he was at the South church when Buford was at North, and vice versa.

Swifty and Arnette were two of my mom and dad's closest friends and biggest supporters during their years of ministry. They volunteered tirelessly at both the Youth Ranch and the church. Just so no one gets the idea that Swifty came up with a feasibility study to say what Buford wanted to hear, I must share the man's background.

Charles Swift was originally from Alexandria, Indiana, where he raced motorcycles as a young man. He moved to Miami in the early 1960s and became a motorcycle cop for the Miami-Dade police force.

In 1964, he was instrumental in solving the murder of a young girl, leading to an arrest and conviction in the case. It was a big story in Miami, and it caught the attention of executives at Gulf Oil, who were looking for a security expert. They were accustomed to hiring ex-FBI agents, but they interviewed Swifty and were impressed enough to hire him to be in charge of security for all Gulf Oil facilities in the Southeastern United States.

The Swifts were relocated to Atlanta, where they immediately resumed a friendship with my parents that had begun before Mom and Dad were even married. They became, like I said, ardent supporters of the ministry, with Swifty serving as Chairman of the Youth Ranch's Board of Directors in its earliest years.

Swifty immediately had his plate full with the new Gulf Oil position. The company was missing several thousand gallons of fuel every month from their tank facility in North Atlanta, and they couldn't figure out where it was going. Swifty took my dad as his assistant, and they pretended to be a survey crew at that bulk tank plant so that Swifty could look around and get a feel for what was going on there. After a few daytime trips to the plant, he purchased a long-focus camera lens and spent many frigid nights during the month of January 1965 at the top of a water tower across the street from the plant. He took pictures of trucks coming in at night and their drivers illegally loading fuel, which they would sell the next day to service stations and pocket the money. Swifty took close-ups of the thieves in action as they stole fuel. He then called them in one by one and asked them if they knew anything about the missing fuel, showing them the pictures he'd taken when they denied knowledge of the theft. Gulf Oil fired approximately twenty-three men due to Swifty's investigation, and it secured his position within the company.

He was transferred to London in the early 1970s, and during those years abroad, he traveled frequently to Africa for Gulf Oil. The company brought him back to the States – to Reston, Virginia, where we visited them during the summer of 1975, and where they were instrumental in starting Reston Bible Church, which is still thriving today. After another transfer, this time to Houston, Texas, Gulf Oil moved the Swifts back to Atlanta in 1979, and they built a house next door to my parents, where they lived for over twenty years.

Swifty and Arnette were active in the church until they moved to Columbia, South Carolina, in 2001 to be near their son and grandchildren. In 2007, my son, Hunter, played in the USTA Junior Tennis Southern Championships (twelve and under division) in Columbia. We drove over from Atlanta the afternoon before Hunter's first match and had dinner that evening with Swifty and Arnette, Rick and his wife, Patty, and their three children. Swifty was in poor health, and he was quiet – not at all like the Swifty I'd known my whole life. I remember thinking when we said goodbye that night that it might have been for the last time.

A few months later, I walked into the church one afternoon to pick my kids up from school, and the receptionist said she had something for me. "An older couple walked in and asked me to give this to you." It was a beautiful handmade lazy Susan with a picture of my home burned into the wood. The sticky note on it said, "To Sandi, From Uncle Swifty."

Swifty passed away in 2009, and we miss him.

Take My Life and Let It Be

Take my life and let it be
Consecrated, Lord, to thee[52]

B uford Horace Adams, Junior (Beau), is not quite as tall as his dad, but they share a similar build. His hair and complexion are lighter than Buford's, closer to that of his mother's. Every bit as good a person as both of his parents, he's a combination of their personalities.

Beau graduated from Morrow High School in 1987, and that fall, he began his freshman year of college at Liberty University in Lynchburg, Virginia.[53] The next year, he transferred to Georgia State University. "I couldn't handle all the rules [at Liberty]. I kept getting fines for dressing wrong. You had to wear a tie to class. You couldn't listen to any music that didn't have Christian lyrics, and I had some, so it cost me a lot of money in fines," he says. "I knew I'd stick it out that year, but then I decided to move back."

---

52 Words by Frances Ridley Havergal
53 Toby Mac, Michael Tait, and Kevin Max Smith, better known as DC Talk, lived down the hall from Beau, and they formed the band during that year at Liberty.

I Am Loved at Community Bible Church

Back in Atlanta, he began looking for a job. He drove to Chick-Fil-A headquarters and asked to see Dan Cathy, one of Truett's sons.

"May I ask why you'd like to see him?" the receptionist said.

"I'm looking for a job."

Impressed by his confidence, Chick-Fil-A hired him and assigned him to package pickup in their mailroom.

Patty and Mike Gumbinger were longtime members of the church who for years had volunteered in the youth ministry. Patty was a special education teacher in the Clayton County school system. She had a close relationship with the Adams, having been the primary babysitter for their children for many years. Mike was a former high school teacher at the Christian school and was the current church administrator. On any given Friday or Saturday night, ten or twenty high-school aged kids would congregate at their house to play cards, eat their pretzels, potato chips, and Cheetos, and drink all their Cokes.

One weekend night, several of those teenagers, most of whom were now in college, were at their house, and the conversation turned to how they missed being in Powerplay, the youth group. Someone suggested that they start a Bible study for college students. Beau was nominated to lead it, and the Gumbingers offered the living room of their new home, which hadn't yet been furnished, for a meeting place.

At the first meeting, Beau sat on the brick hearth of their fireplace and delivered a short devotional to his fellow college students, who sat scattered around on the living room floor. Bit by bit, people started offering to play the guitar and sing. After the meetings, students played ping pong in the basement or sat around the kitchen table playing cards and talking. The setting and structure were vaguely reminiscent of the early Youth Ranch days. Within just a few months, the Bible study became a gathering place for not only Georgia State students but also Clayton State College (formerly Clayton Junior College) students. The group soon outgrew the Gumbinger's living room. The Bible study moved to the Powerplay building on Reynolds Road, and the church offered Beau a part-time position as College pastor in 1989.

"For me, that was my first real exposure to the inner workings of the church, from the standpoint of having to go to staff meetings and working to grow the College ministry," he says. "I also began to think that maybe this ministry thing might be my gig."

As for his college studies, he was beginning to doubt that he liked his major -- psychology -- enough to focus on it for the rest of his life. Switching his major to communications, he reasoned, would do two things: first, it would teach him how to be an effective public speaker, a skill he knew would be valuable no matter what vocation he chose, and second, a degree in communications required fewer math courses. "I decided this is the way I gotta go," he says, laughing.

The Bible study continued to grow, and they gave it a name: Off-Campus Bible Study, OCBS for short. New musicians joined the band, and students came from not only Georgia State and Clayton State but also Georgia Tech and Gordon College in Barnesville. By 1991, close to three hundred college students were attending the weekly meetings.

One afternoon around that time, Beau ran into a high school buddy. Jimmy Nidifer had played on the soccer team at Morrow High School with Beau. He was a couple of years ahead of Beau, so they weren't close friends, but Beau says everyone who knew soccer in Clayton County knew the Nidifer family. Jimmy and his cousin were the stars on that Morrow High School team. The day he saw Jimmy, Beau told him that he led a Bible study and invited him to OCBS. Jimmy thanked him for the invitation but graciously declined, saying he really didn't think he needed God. He just wanted to have a good time and live his life his way. In fact, he told Beau, he had a big weekend planned in Panama City Beach.

Just a few nights after that conversation, Beau got a phone call from another friend who had played on that high school soccer team. He was calling to tell Beau that Jimmy Nidifer and his cousin had been killed in a car crash on their way home from Florida. The boy's words -- "I'm just going to live my life my way and have fun" – rang in Beau's ears.

When Beau graduated from Georgia State in 1991, he was still unsure about being cut out for the pastorate. He wanted to sort it out in his head, and he knew that if God was, indeed, leading him into the ministry, he would need more preparation. He applied for a six-month Bible course at Capernwray, the Torchbearers school in England started by Major Ian Thomas, the man who had spent so much time in the Adams's home during his childhood.

"I flew into London, and I didn't know a soul over there. I landed, and I was supposed to get to northern England. I rode a train from the airport to downtown London, and I walked out of the train station thinking there had to be a hotel where I could stay. I found this little bed and breakfast, and this lady took me up the stairs to a tiny room." After he'd unpacked his bags, he decided that he needed to see London. It was still early in the morning when he set out on a walk. He got to St. James Park, not far from Buckingham Palace, and sat down on a park bench to take in the beauty. "The next thing I know, it was four hours later, and I was like, oh my God, I'm here in London sleeping on a bench!"

Take My Life and Let It Be

After a full day of exploring the city, he made his way back to the little hotel and went to bed. But he was so jetlagged, he remembers waking up in the middle of the night thinking *what have I done?*" The next morning, he pulled himself together and found a train that would take him to Carnforth in Lancashire, on the northwestern coast of England. A taxi delivered him to the front entrance of an old castle that was Capernwray Hall.

His dorm room in that old castle had walls covered in black mildew and was sparsely furnished with just the essentials – bunk beds and desks. His roommates were boys from Canada and from Israel.

The principal of Capernwray at the time was a short Scottish man with a thick Glasgow accent named Billy Strachan. Strachan was a practical jokester who dressed in kilts for special occasions and loved to perform magic tricks. He was also the teacher who would turn out to be most influential in Beau's life.

At times, Strachan would address the entire student body, yet Beau's roommates would turn to Beau and say, "He was really just talking to you then."

Beau says, "It was bizarre because they were students there, too. But it happened more than once." He specifically remembers Strachan saying, "One day, you're going to be a pastor, and you're going to be exhausted and worn out and saying that you just can't do it anymore, and then you're going to remember the words of an old Scottish preacher who told you it's Christ in you that CAN do it, and you need to relax."

With students from seventy different countries in attendance, Capernwray greatly expanded Beau's worldview. And it provided some necessary time for contemplation. When he wasn't working on campus or sitting in class, Beau took long walks to a nearby mountain, past flocks of sheep grazing on impossibly green grass and fenced in by old stone walls. "For me, that trip was transformational," he says. "That's where I felt like I got God's vision for my life. I would sit on that mountain and look out to the ocean and ask God, 'What do you want me to do?'"

In January 1992, during one of Beau's calls to home, Buford told him that the church's youth minister had resigned. The church needed to replace him immediately. "Think about it," his dad said, "and let me know if you're willing to come back and do the youth ministry here at the church." Beau wrestled with the decision for about a week. He loved Capernwray, and he didn't quite feel ready to go home. He still had a few months left in the term. But he wondered if this wasn't God's answer to his direct question of what God wanted him to do.

When he'd made his decision, Beau went to Strachan to tell him he was leaving. The man questioned him carefully about his plans but never tried to convince him to stay. "It was as if he already knew I was going," Beau says.

One of girls on staff at the school drove him to the train station. Once in London, he purchased his return ticket to Atlanta. He boarded that flight back to the United States, not knowing that one day he would return to train pastors in this country where he had received his training.

At long last, I have the chance to tell my side of a story that Beau has been telling in church for several years.

Patty Saenger (now Gumbinger) joined the church in the mid-1970s, and she became our regular babysitter not long after that. One night when I was probably nine, Beau seven, and Holly three, Patty was watching us so that our parents could go out for the evening. Patty promised that after dinner, she would take us to Dairy Queen.

She was cleaning up the kitchen when Beau walked into the family room and lay down on the sofa, saying his stomach hurt. No one paid much attention to that until Patty announced it was time to go get an ice cream, and Beau said he didn't want to go.

I remember sitting in the living room trying to coax him off the sofa. He was having none of it, and that's when Patty realized he was really sick. Then he began moaning and clutching his side. Patty said, "I wonder if he's got appendicitis."

On the long paneled family room wall next to the fireplace was a pair of wooden shelves made from rough-sawn cedar that Opa had constructed for my mom. I walked over and pulled the A volume of our set of *World Book* encyclopedias off the shelf and leafed through it until I found the entry for "appendicitis." I can't remember the exact words in that entry, but I read aloud to Patty that the way to determine if someone had appendicitis was to draw an invisible line from the navel to the hipbone and find the spot roughly halfway between the two. Press on the spot with two fingers, and if the patient reacts, it is most likely appendicitis, the encyclopedia instructed.

I walked over to the sofa and stood over Beau. Holding the encyclopedia in my left hand, I reached down and, with the index and middle fingers of my right hand, pressed on the magic spot. Beau howled. I turned around to Patty and said, "I think he has appendicitis."

She found my parents, who came racing home. They put Beau into the car, and on the way to Clayton General Hospital, he vomited in Mom's purse (another symptom of appendicitis). He had an emergency appendectomy that evening, and most likely, he got ice cream in the hospital the next day. Holly and I spent the night with Patty.

Now, nearly forty years later, my brother's version is that I was angry because we couldn't get an ice cream so I walked over to him and punched him in the stomach. And that simply is not true. Although I would do just about anything for a Peanut Buster Parfait, I would never punch my brother over one.

He's Got the Whole World in His Hands

He's got you and me, brother, in his hands
He's got you and me, sister, in his hands,
He's got the whole world in his hands[54]

The same week he returned from England, Beau moved into the Powerplay building's apartment and started his new job as the church's youth pastor. He recruited several young men who had kept Off-Campus Bible study running during his absence to help with the youth ministry. Jody Shaw, Glenn Sanders, Daryl Sanders, Greg McGaha, Clark Johnson, Michael Wilder, and Unity Nkosi – all college students at the time -- worked tirelessly as volunteers. It's probably not surprising that some of these men are still in the ministry today.

One night while was speaking at the Bible study, Beau noticed a couple of girls he'd never seen before walk through the back door. After the meeting, he introduced himself and invited the girls to come back. "I still remember what she was wearing," he says of one, a Riverdale High School graduate named Kim

---

54 Traditional spiritual

Bradley, a dark-haired beauty whose eyes crinkled shut when she smiled. It wasn't long before the two were dating, and they were married September 25, 1993, in the Reynolds Road auditorium.[55]

When the South campus first opened in 1992, much of the church's administration was still conducted from the Morrow location. Although Buford moved his office to the Stockbridge campus (just like it had been on Reynolds Road, it was next door to the baby nursery), most of the church's daily activities still took place at the North campus.

Gradually, the church's various ministries began to open branches at the South location. AWANA was able to squeeze a game circle into the church's foyer. The new club began meeting on Thursday evenings, while the old club continued to meet on Wednesdays in the Reynolds Road gymnasium. And although most of the ministries thrived, a few struggled, mostly because of a lack of space.

The South campus building only had a handful of rooms, and those were used for nurseries and children's Sunday school, so there was no available space for adult Sunday school classes. Years of ministry had taught Buford and Jack that a large church that failed to find ways for its members to connect with others in small groups would not grow. People would eventually drift away if they didn't feel like they belonged.

The church was not yet in the financial position to build another building, so they had to think creatively in order to figure out a way for adult Sunday school classes to meet. They came up with the idea of asking people who lived within a mile or so of the church to host Sunday school classes in their homes. After

---

55 Their son, Chase, was born July 12, 1995. Madison arrived eleven months later, on June 14, 1996.

the 9:30 service ended, adults left the campus and went to one of several different host homes. Then, when the church's growth made those homes insufficient to fill the need, the church rented space in the county's newest high school, Eagle's Landing High, and several new classes began meeting there.

In 1995, the church raised $1 million in contribution pledges for a classroom building. They took those pledges to Bank South, the same bank holding the $3 million mortgage on the auditorium building, and borrowed the money to construct a classroom building. Again, Darrel Rutherford was hired as the architect. The contract with him was signed September 7, 1995. Construction was completed in 1996, giving that South campus the Sunday school and Awana space it so desperately needed.

Another ministry that initially did not thrive at the South location was the youth ministry. Church leadership believed its struggle to be a function of where they were meeting – the church's choir room. Beau looked around for alternative meeting sites that the church could afford, and they began renting the old American Legion building just off of the square in McDonough, about seven miles from the church. Soon they had teenagers coming from all three high schools in Henry County–Stockbridge High School, Henry County High in McDonough and the brand-new Eagle's Landing High, which was just down the road from the church.[56] Buford and Beau began to explore the possibility of constructing a separate Powerplay building at the Jodeco Road location.

The history of Community Bible Church and all of its ministries has often been summarized as this: a cast of unlikely characters being used by God to accomplish great things. By the

---

56 As of January 2014, Henry County's school system had grown to 10 high schools.

mid-1990s, that cast of characters had grown to include one or two crooked politicians, a state senator, a crotchety judge, a used-car salesman, and a nuclear physicist. In 1997, a tragedy would add a wealthy bar owner to the list.

Toney Jones, one of the original Youth Ranch kids and the man who had taken over leadership of the Youth Ranch in the early 1970s so that Buford could focus on pastoring the church, had drifted a long way from the ministry and from the Lord. He'd left his wife and children. He still lived in Clayton County, and he owned six bars in the area. Although he never came to church, every once in a while he dropped by the church office to leave a bag full of dollar bills collected from vending machines in his bars, always asking that the money be used for the youth ministry.

Toney's eighteen-year-old son, Jeremiah, was killed in 1995. A heartbroken Toney went to see Buford. "I want teens to have the opportunity I had growing up," he said, handing him a large amount of cash and adding, "If Jeremiah had been in Youth Ranch, this wouldn't have happened."

When he admitted that the money had come from the bar business and wondered if the church would even want it, Buford said something vaguely reminiscent of what the banker Pierce Peacock had said to him years earlier: "The devil's had that money long enough. Let's do something good with it."

With Toney's gift and a great deal of volunteer labor, the church constructed a building on the far western corner of the Jodeco Road property. On a beautiful April Saturday in 1997, the church held another "barn-raising," and the building was almost completely framed in one day. The Jeremiah Justice Youth Center was completed and dedicated in the memory of Jeremiah Jones in 1997. "That was the greatest compliment I could ever have," Toney says.

In 1999, that building was expanded to nearly double its original size, thanks to the generous offer of longtime church members to match dollar-for-dollar up to $50,000 the amount raised for its renovation.

A year after I graduated from Georgia State University with a degree in English and Journalism, my dad called to say that the church's publications director was moving away, and he offered me the position.

My first day on the job, I was introduced to a new computer that they assured me would be very easy to learn. It was a Mac SE, one of Apple's earliest models. It had a screen that was about four inches square, and the desktop publishing software was an early version of Aldus PageMaker. By the end of my first day, I was in love with my job. I'd worked summers in the church office throughout high school and college, occasionally assisting with production of the church's weekly bulletin. The Mac and PageMaker revolutionized that process.

After I had my first child, Morgan, in August 1990, the church allowed me to do most of my work from home. My responsibilities included the writing, layout, and design of every piece of printed material produced by the church – Sunday bulletins, the twice-monthly church newsletter called *Perspective*, stewardship materials, and Missions Conference materials were the big publications – plus church promotions and public relations. I was incredibly lucky to have a job that allowed me to use my college degree on a daily basis and to be able to keep that job and still stay at home with my children.[57]

In the fall of 1990, the *Clayton News/Daily* did a two-page spread on the church's twenty-fifth anniversary and my parents' thirty years in ministry. In it, the writer, Jeff Whitfield, pointed out that during the 1980s, the church had nearly doubled its membership and had more than doubled its budget. Whitfield ended the article with these words:

> The vision of the Adams' has likely expanded far beyond what they imagined when they first started in the youth ministry 25 years ago. The world has changed from "Father Knows Best" to "The Simpsons" and more than ever does society need churches and leaders who care enough to want to make a difference and who have the vision to work on the present while planning for the future.[58]

After this article was published, Whitfield, who was the paper's religion editor, asked Dad to write a monthly column in its Religion section. As an aspiring writer who had taken several newspaper and magazine writing classes, I was thrilled because I knew I would get to help. I had long admired Lewis Grizzard, the nationally syndicated humor columnist at the *Atlanta Journal-Constitution*, so being able to work on a newspaper column was a dream come true for me.

Dad dictated those columns into a portable tape recorder, and then I transcribed and edited them before sending them to the paper. The following is one that became a reader favorite:

---

57 Morgan (August 1990), Lauren (February 1993), and Hunter (July 1995)

58 *(Clayton News/Daily, Oct. 1, 1990)*

How to Impress the Preacher

My parents live in a house well over 100 years old on my mom's old home place in Texas Valley. Texas Valley is just outside the small town of Armuchee, which is north of Rome, Georgia. Although the folks up there do have electricity and running water, we are talking real country here.

The next home place down from them belongs to my cousins, Tim and Tilda, who are in their seventies. Although Tim doesn't go to church much, he wants to make a good impression anytime they get a new pastor.

Back in the early spring, Antioch Baptist Church, where everyone in the Valley attends, called a new pastor, and Tim let it be known that he wanted the new preacher to come by. Tim's philosophy is you never know when you are going to die. Since the preacher will have to do the funeral, he needs to at least have met you.

Texas Valley is adjacent to about 30,000 acres belonging to Berry College. The school forbids hunting on its property, so thousands of deer migrate off of that property and into the gardens of folks in the Valley. They have to take extraordinary measure to protect their gardens – fences, sometimes even electric fences, and the occasional shotgun blast – to scare the deer away.

One cold, windy Saturday morning, Tim worked in his garden to repair the damage the deer had done the night before. After he had finished, he went inside to take a warm shower. Just as he was lathering up, he heard his dog barking outside, that particular bark that usually indicated the deer were again in the garden.

Tim was furious. He jumped out of the shower, grabbed his shotgun, and headed out the back door completely in the buff and ready to scare away the deer.

There were no deer. The preacher had come "calling." Now Tilda, who is just a bit sadistic, saw the whole situation – Tim in the buff standing on the back porch with his shotgun, shivering by now, and the preacher at the front door. She played it for all it was worth.

She said in a loud voice, "Come on in, preacher, and sit down. Let me make a pot of coffee, and we can sit and chat a while," knowing that Tim couldn't get back into the house because the back door was completely visible from the living room. So for an hour, Tilda sat and visited with the preacher while Tim stood shivering and miserable on the back porch, shotgun in hand.

It's funny what people will do to make a good impression. As a pastor, I have seen big, strong men stuff open beer cans between couch cushions and sit on them trying to make a good impression on me.

I've rung doorbells and seen someone peek through the curtains only to hear strange noises within the house like folks were suddenly moving to Phoenix. A couple of minutes later, someone invites me into the house, and I wonder what or maybe even who has been stuffed into the closets.

It's amazing, isn't it? I'm no one's judge. I have enough baggage in my own life – more than enough, in fact – to keep me busy. So why should I try to figure out whether someone else is measuring up to another's arbitrary standard? Ultimately, we will all stand before the One who is able to judge righteously, and the only standing we will have is our relationship based on His grace and forgiveness.

Every time I am tempted to put on airs or put my best foot forward or to try to impress someone, an image of Tim standing on his back porch shivering in the cold March wind flashes through my mind.

Putting on the dog can sure get you in the doghouse.

Another part of my job was preparing an outline of Dad's sermon each week for publication in the Sunday bulletin. At some point every Tuesday morning, Dad would walk into my office and lay a 5 ½ by 8 ½ inch sheet of paper on my desk. On it would be his notes for the next Sunday's sermon, written in his half-cursive, half-print handwriting and crammed to fit on that half sheet because it was perfectly sized to fit inside his Bible. The major points would be highlighted so that I knew what to include in the bulletin outline. I was always amazed at how adept Dad was at boiling down a 45-minute sermon into, well, three points and a poem. For instance, on December 10, 1989, the sermon was titled "The Wisdom of the Wise Men." The three main points of the sermon were 1. Wise in the Way They Sought Jesus; 2. Wise in the Way They Were Taught of Him; and 3. Wise in What They Brought Him. The "poem" could have been an actual poem or maybe a short anecdote about what's important at Christmastime. Or something he heard on Paul Harvey's "The Rest of The Story." Or he might have opened with a line such as, "Like a chicken laying an egg in traffic, I'm going to lay it on the line and do it quickly," a joke intended to elicit a laugh while reassuring people that he would end the sermon on time. No matter what the hook he used to begin his messages, Dad always stayed on point, and he never went one minute past twelve o'clock on Sunday morning, mostly because he was as ready for lunch as every other person in the sanctuary!

Because it was part of preparing the layout for the weekly bulletin, typing the Sunday Sermon Notes was an aspect of the job I enjoyed. But the part I detested also involved Dad's sermon notes. One of Dad's first requests when I started working full-time at the church was that I design a foolproof index system for his past sermons, which to that point were haphazardly housed in a metal file cabinet in a tiny, windowless room behind my office.

Although he reused jokes and illustrations, Dad never preached the exact same sermon twice. He did cut and paste texts and major points to create new messages during the thirty-plus years he preached. And to do that, he needed to be able to locate past sermons on related subjects.

I began by creating a list of key words that corresponded to file folders in that cabinet headed with the same names. So, for instance, if Dad did a message on the family using Ephesians 5 and 6 as his text, I could go to the computer, type in the words "Ephesians" or "family," "husbands, "wives," or "children," and locate every sermon he'd ever preached on the topic. Or "The Wisdom of the Wise Men" sermon would have been listed under "Christmas" and possibly under "wisdom" (in case he remembered the title and wanted to search for it that way).

Of course, it wasn't a foolproof system. I can't begin to count the number of times Dad would rifle through those file folders and inevitably come out of that back office with his hands in the air, saying, "Why can't we figure out a way to do this?" Then I'd walk back there and find the sermon on the topic of family from Ephesians filed under "Mother's Day" because he'd last used it in May two years before under the title "Gifts for Mom."

He's Got the Whole World in His Hands

Thanks to Steve Jobs and the iPad, my brother has a much better sermon filing system than Dad ever did. Beau keeps every sermon on his iPad, and all he has to do is type in a keyword to find a previous message. It's the system I envisioned nearly thirty years ago, only this one works.

When the Roll Is Called
Up Yonder, I'll Be There

Let us labor for the Master
from the dawn till setting sun,
Let us talk of all His wondrous love and care;
Then when all of life is over,
and our work on earth is done,
And when the roll is called up yonder, I'll be there.[59]

Constructed in 1936 on Techwood Drive near Georgia Tech University, Techwood homes was the first public housing project ever built in the United States. It was demolished in 1995, partly because of Atlanta's preparations for the 1996 Summer Olympics.

In fact, between 1995 and 2010, every public housing project in Atlanta was demolished as a result of a plan titled HOPE VI, which was enacted under President Bill Clinton as a way of dispersing residents from centralized projects. The plan was initially proposed because public housing projects across the nation had become so crime-ridden. Under HOPE VI, local housing authorities would receive grants for revitalizing public housing. The plan was to build new developments in their

---

59 Words and music by James M. Black

place that would attract higher-income renters while providing those in poverty with Section 8[60] vouchers that would enable them to live in the same new complexes. The idea, and it was a sound one, was that breaking up the pockets or concentrations of poverty would reduce crime rates.

When it was enacted in 1992, HOPE VI mandated that for every public housing unit demolished, one new unit of public housing had to be built. But in 1995, that one-for-one replacement requirement for HOPE VI funding was repealed. The Atlanta Housing Authority quickly proposed tearing down Techwood Homes and nearby Clark Howell Homes (1,195 housing units in total) and replacing them with a mixed-use development of only 900 housing units. Atlanta jumped on HOPE VI because it was preparing for the Olympics and wanted to "clean up" the housing projects by the time the world came to visit. The plan passed, and both projects were torn down.

Where did those 295 displaced households go? While the Atlanta Housing Authority adamantly denies that those families left the city, it also admits that it did not keep track of residents who were displaced by the demolition of Techwood Homes in 1995. Nor did they follow residents who moved out of Atlanta's public housing during the next fifteen years, when the remaining projects in Atlanta were demolished to make way for mixed-use developments.

A 2008 article in *Creative Loafing* titled "Clayton County's Tribulations" disputes the claim that those residents didn't leave

---

60 Section 8 was created as part of the Housing and Community Development Act of 1974, an amendment to the U.S. Housing Act of 1937. Under Section 8, tenants pay approximately thirty percent of their income for rent, and the balance of the monthly rental fee is paid by the federal government.

the city. "Data from the Atlanta Regional Commission show that from 2000 to 2005, 94,698 people migrated [to Clayton County] from the 20-county metro region. Nearly half of them moved from Fulton County . . . And while new, poorer residents were moving in, many longtime Clayton residents began an exodus to neighboring counties such as Fayette, Spalding and Henry," writes author Tomas Wheatley.[61]

Perhaps one reason low-income families chose Clayton County was that it historically has had the lowest sales tax rate of any county in metro Atlanta. Another goes back to Section 8's Housing Choice Voucher Program, which allowed those qualifying for housing assistance to use their vouchers to purchase homes. In the *Creative Loafing* article, Kem Kimbrough, an Emory law school graduate and former sheriff of Clayton County, is quoted as saying, "You could buy one heck of a house and not only were you going to get a bargain on the house and the size and the yard, but the taxes would be low. The economy seemed to be booming, and Clayton County had it going on. There was a significant air that Clayton County was the place of opportunity."

Community Bible Church leadership had no way of knowing in 1996 that HOPE VI might affect Clayton County. But they had witnessed firsthand the decline of several large churches in the outskirts of Atlanta due to the economic downturn of the areas surrounding those churches. They grew increasingly concerned, for while it is important for churches to minister to the "poorest of these," churches in the late twentieth and early twenty-first centuries rely on two things for their livelihood: contributions and

---

61 In 2007, a Clayton County grand jury requested a study to determine what kind of strain those new residents were putting on local resources. See "Grand Jury Reveals Concerns About Influx of New Residents." *Atlanta-Journal Constitution*, 2/15/07

tuition from daycare and/or private schools. In impoverished neighborhoods, large churches cannot expect large contributions unless they retain wealthy members willing to commute from their upscale neighborhoods. In addition, their school and day-care enrollments will suffer because parents able to afford private school tuition most often choose schools near their homes and ones they deem to be safer environments for their children.

Jack Bartlett puts it a bit more succinctly: "Where would we be today if we hadn't moved to Henry County? We were faced with three choices back then – we could stay where we were and de-cline, we could stay and try to survive by changing who we were, or we could move and do what we'd always done well."

By 1996, the majority of the church's membership lived in Henry County, and the pastors were weary from the strain of what was, essentially, doing their jobs in two places. Most alarmingly, though, the North campus offerings were no longer adequate to cover that location's operating expenses. The South church was subsidizing the North campus. While the argument could have been made that it was only fair, since the North church had essen-tially given birth to the South one, the Jodeco Road location could not afford to support the Clayton County campus and add more needed building space. Having two churches that were unable to grow spelled disaster for the entire ministry. Buford called an Elders' meeting to discuss their options.

Buford says of that meeting, "We realized that, as a whole entity, the church was not going to survive if we continued to have to support the North church from the South church. Kent Kelso was the chairman, and he began the meeting by saying that we were not going to make any decision unless it was a unanimous one. We had a long discussion that night, and ulti-mately it came down to a vote on whether or not we would sell the North church. It was a unanimous decision, and one of the board members, Norm Wood, a retired military guy, said he would be glad to craft the resolution."

Within a few days, the board called a congregational meeting. It was set for Sunday, March 17, 1996, during the evening service at the North campus. Normally on Sunday nights, church crowds are sparse. But on this night, because word had gotten out that Buford was going to announce the closing of the North church, members almost had to be wedged into the pews with shoehorns.

By that night, two or three Elders, including the man who had crafted the resolution, had felt the heat of the congregation and had changed their minds. While the majority of the board was still resolved to sell the church, there were a few dissident members.

The Elders filed into the auditorium and sat across the stage behind Buford, whose job it was to announce the decision and then take questions. The majority of the crowd was supportive, understanding that the Elders had made what they felt was a necessary economic decision, something that had to be done for the church to survive. Nevertheless, several people were terribly upset over the announcement.

Buford says, "They just didn't like the idea that times were changing and that the church was changing. They were very vocal and very accusatory. I stood there probably for an hour answering their questions, and it really was an ugly experience."

Hesitating as if to choose his words carefully, he continues, "I was surrounded by a crowd of people pointing fingers in my face, accusing me of being a traitor. In the middle of it all, Beau came up and said, 'Dad, Mom needs you.' I didn't realize the urgency of the situation, so I kept answering questions. Finally, he grabbed me by the arm and said, 'Dad, Mom needs you right now.' He pulled me out of the crowd, and we walked down the hall to a nursery room, where Babs was on the floor crying uncontrollably."

When the service ended, seeing Buford immediately surrounded by a group of people and feeling the anger in the room, Babs left quickly through a side door with the intention of waiting in Buford's office for him to finish answering questions. But as she walked down the hallway toward his office, she was confronted by some angry members who wanted to vent their frustrations. It was unfair, to be sure, because she hadn't been part of the discussions on selling the North church property. Neither had she had an official vote on the night the Elders made that decision. She tried explaining to those blocking her path that she wasn't the one with whom they had a quarrel, but the more she tried to get away, the more irate and accusatory they became. Desperate, she turned and ran into an empty nursery room and collapsed on the floor in tears. Mike and Sandi Reid, longtime friends who had been on their way to Buford's office to express their support, witnessed the confrontation from down the hallway and rushed to comfort her.

Buford says, "Babs had felt the pressure of the meeting and the energy in the room far more than I had. I think that night both of us decided it's just not worth it to go through this in your life when people you think you're helping and serving and ministering to, when they can be so angry and accuse you of the things they're accusing you of when you really wanted to be there doing good."

The next morning, Buford wrote the longest letter he had ever written to the church membership. And this one did not begin with the typical "Dear Folks" greeting he had used for over twenty-five years. What follows is the full text of that letter:

Dear Fellow Community Bible Church Members both North and South,

I am writing to communicate to you a decision unanimously reached by the board of elders and the reasons behind that decision.

This was communicated Sunday evening, March 17, at North Church, but for those members who were unable to attend and for all South church members it is important that we all have accurate information to combat any rumors that might arise. First the decision:

UNIFICATION RESOLUTION

After much prayer and many hours of open and honest discussion, we, the Board of Elders of Community Bible Church, unanimously agree to the following action to insure the continued spiritual growth and health of Community Bible Church. Be it resolved that September 8, 1996, will be designated as Homecoming Sunday. On that day Community Bible Church will be permanently unified as one and join in worship services and Sunday school at 2001 Jodeco Road. We believe that this reuniting of our congregations will bring strength and unity and enable us to pursue our ongoing vision: To worship and evangelize our community and equip the saints for ministry.

Now, the reasons behind the decision necessitate that we review a little of our history. About six years ago, we were maxed out in both auditorium services and two Sunday schools on Reynolds Road. We had acquired twenty-nine acres north of the church and were seriously considering building educational space near the corner of Reynolds and Huie Roads. This would later lead us to construct a new sanctuary at the same corner and ultimately require that we move our entire complex about a half a mile up Reynolds Road from where it presently is. As we considered this option, we realized it would take years to fulfill, and we also realized that we would be spending millions of dollars to accommodate our growing congregation. There was no space available immediately next to our present buildings. Flood plain laws made it unwise to even consider building even across the street. We also began to notice that more and more of our membership lived south of Georgia Highway 138. All of this led us to raise the question, would it be better to build several miles south of our present location rather than just a half-mile up the road? Ultimately, we decided to look for land in Henry County and build there to accommodate the membership that had already moved to that area. We would be "one church in two places." This model had been tried by Briarwood Presbyterian in Birmingham, First Baptist Church of Atlanta, and Mount Paran Church of God. As we prayed and sought the Lord's face, this seemed to be His will. Of course, you know that we did build in Henry County, and about 300 of our church members elected to begin attending church there. During the last three years, that church has grown rapidly while at the same time North church attendance has steadily declined.

After operating for over three years in two locations, it has become apparent that we cannot continue in this fashion indefinitely for a number of reasons. First, the staff is stretched too thin and after three years is beyond the point of being exhausted. It has become almost impossible to give adequate ministry to both congregations. This is true in our youth ministry, in the music ministry and the general pastoring of the church, frankly, in all areas. Secondly, building maintenance and utilities from two sets of buildings is a far greater expense than we originally anticipated. As the buildings in Morrow grow older, major expenditures are necessary. Thirdly, the leadership of Community Bible senses that the two congregations are becoming more and more divergent. It is becoming more difficult for the common leadership that we share to keep both congregations focused and moving in the same direction. Fourth, we have always had as our purpose to worship, evangelize, and train leaders for ministry. This purpose is increasingly being lost in the struggle for unity and for survival. The leadership of the church feels it is critical that we get back to what we do best, evangelizing in a growing community.

Both the elders and the staff share the responsibility and accept the responsibility for the position that we are in. Literally thousands of churches face this situation and it is important to realize that there are not good guys and bad guys here, it is simply a dilemma that a church can find itself in. How do you minister in a changing community? What are your options? In order to refocus our vision on ministry, in order to reunite the congregation under one purpose statement and with one vision, we feel that now is the time to begin meeting again under one roof. That is the reason for the decision to reunite the congregations at the South church location

You might have read that Henry County is now among the ten fastest growing counties in the United States of America.

When the Roll Is Called Up Yonder, I'll Be There

There is an incredible opportunity before us to do the work of evangelism. Literally thousands of young couples are moving into starter homes all around the South church and it is our job to reach out and share the gospel with them. Let me emphasize just a couple other important items.

It is critical that every North church member realize that they are needed and wanted at the South church. You are the reason for our existence. The members of the North church gave birth to the South church and I can promise you, as pastor, the South church members will welcome you with open arms and open hearts. If you are teaching we need you to continue teaching, if you are working in Awana we need you to continue working in Awana. Whatever job you are doing, whether it is ushering, greeting, singing or whatever, we need you to continue doing exactly that at South church. It is not a matter of making a place for you, you already have a place and a position and a ministry. We need for you to continue doing your job.

It is also important to remember that we are only talking about buildings and geography here. The important things remain the same. The important thing is relationship with the Lord and relationships with each other. The sum total of the law is that we are to love God and love each other. Where we worship is not important but the investment that you have made in relationships in ministry over the years at North church is absolutely critical. Please do not walk away from ministry and relationships over an inanimate, unimportant issue like a building.

Please remember that even though you, as a North church member, might not agree with the decision the elders reached, they reached it after much prayer, it was a unanimous decision with both the North and South church elders agreeing and, as the leadership of the church, we ask that you at least give it a chance. If your first inclination is to say, "I have to find me another church, my church is closing," your conclusion is simply wrong. Your church is not closing, it is just moving down the highway 12 miles. The same people will be doing the same things in the same positions and relationships will stay intact. Please give it a chance, try it for three months. At the end of that time if the Lord has not given you peace about it or you do not feel comfortable, then that is the time to make a decision. But do not make a decision in the heat of the emotion to sever relationships.

Finally, to the South church members let me emphasize that the people that are coming from the North church are our predecessors. We owe much to them. We need to be ready to make any accommodation necessary, whether it is changing the hour we worship, changing the Sunday school class we are in or whatever, in order to give them preference in our worship services. They have sacrificed much for us, it is time for us to sacrifice for them. I know you will have that spirit of oneness and love as we reunite.

As your pastor, let me just call on the church as a whole to keep the main thing the main thing. We are here to worship God, to do the work of evangelism and to encourage and equip each other for the ministry. That is what is important. Everything else just amounts to detail. We have an opportunity before us that is literally beyond belief. We have a beautiful location in one of the fastest growing communities in America, we have a strong and vibrant congregation and, as we join forces, we can become an incredibly strong ministry. We can truly be salt and light for all of the South Metro area.

When the Roll Is Called Up Yonder, I'll Be There

We realize that big changes like this can cause folks to go through a time of shock, disbelief, grief, anger, fear and a whole array of other emotions. Both the elders and the staff are committed to be here to answer your questions and do all that we can to make this a smooth transition.

Your fellow servant,

Buford

P.S. For those interested in a question and answer session, we will have meetings on Wednesday nights at 7:00 in the Chapel of the North church for 3 weeks beginning March 20.

Three weeks later, several church members residing in Clayton County received a letter from a church on Main Street in Forest Park sympathizing with the loss of their church and urging them to visit this particular church. The letter had one particularly offensive line: "As people who are more committed to Jesus Christ than to any particular location or building, we know that you will quickly find a place to settle in and continue to impact this community for Him."

Buford immediately fired off a response to the church's pastor that said, "In all my 30 years of ministry, I have never had another pastor use my church roll as their mailing list in an obvious attempt to proselytize our membership." It went on to ask that the pastor call him so that they could sit down and discuss the issue, but Buford never received a response from the man.

The move was completed over the next several months, and on September 8, 1996, the church met in one location for the first time in four years. Buford estimates that nearly one third of the

Clayton congregation chose not to worship in Stockbridge. "So out of about 2500 members, we lost eight or nine hundred members that week. It was the world's fastest declining church for a week or two," he says, adding, "but we quickly picked up that many and more in the South location."

The most vocal opposition to the move did not come from the ones most affected by it. Initially, the church offered transportation for members in Clayton County who wanted to attend the Henry church so that no one – particularly elderly members unable to make the commute – would be left in the cold. Many, like Horace and Glennis Adams and Jack Bartlett's mother, Lois Watkins, went ahead and made the drive themselves. Plenty of those opposing the move lived in Henry County themselves, but in voicing their opposition, they said they believed the church was abandoning those to whom God had called them to minister in Clayton County and vowed to stay at 5900 Reynolds Road.

While I've always believed that the church split of 1982 was the most emotionally trying time for my Dad as a pastor, I think the years of driving between the two churches were hard on him physically. Preaching three forty-five minute sermons consecutively is hard enough without the challenge of a twelve-mile commute between the services. At one point, the rumor around Henry County was that he kept a private helicopter in Eagle's Landing Country Club to transport him between church campuses. But the truth was that he put a lot of miles on his little Mazda Miata during that time.

I got a call from my mom one Sunday morning in the fall of 1993 that, for me, punctuated the stress my dad was under.

When the Roll Is Called Up Yonder, I'll Be There

Dad still got up very early on Sunday mornings, but on this day, he had passed out while getting dressed. Mom was wakened from a deep sleep by a loud crash. She rushed in to their walk-in closet to find him unconscious on the floor. She called 911, and although he had regained consciousness by the time the ambulance arrived, he was bleeding from a cut on his nose. Mom insisted that he go to the hospital.

I was terrified when I got that call from my mom saying they were at the hospital. Imagining that my dad had suffered a heart attack or a stroke, I threw on some clothes and raced over to Henry General.[62] My brother and sister and I sat in the cold plastic chairs in that waiting room, and while a television over our heads played the 2 *Stupid Dogs* cartoon, we debated the possibilities.

It wasn't the first time he'd passed out. In 1989 and 1990, there had been three episodes. The first time, he was at his usual early Sunday morning spot, the Waffle House, when he landed face-first in his breakfast and woke to find several people standing over him. The second episode happened again on a Sunday morning, this time at the Bob Evans restaurant in Morrow. And the third time happened during breakfast one morning in New Orleans while he was at his residency for seminary.

At the time, his doctor was puzzled. Dad was in good physical shape. For years, he'd run five or six miles every weekday. In addition, his heart function was good, and they couldn't pinpoint a common cause for the three incidents, which all happened early in the morning before he was to stand up and speak. Yet he'd been doing that for years without incident. Then the episodes stopped just as abruptly as they'd begun. We all breathed a sigh of relief and chalked it up to stress.

---

62 Now Piedmont Henry hospital

Three years later, when the episodes returned, we were shaken. Yes, it was another Sunday morning before church, but he'd also passed out a couple of months before while they were on vacation in St. Augustine, Florida. In theory, that was a stress-free morning. And on top of all that, each of these latest episodes had resulted in minor injuries.

We were relieved later that morning when the emergency room doctors at Henry General ruled out both a heart attack and stroke. They listened to my mom describe his previous fainting episodes, and they ordered a tilt test to see if they could recreate the conditions under which he lost consciousness. Ultimately, doctors determined that he was experiencing vasovagal syncope, which is basically a response to some sort of trigger in which the vagus nerve, which runs all the way from the brain stem to the colon, somehow is over-stimulated and then causes the body's blood vessels to dilate and the heart to slow down. This makes it hard for the heart to pump blood up to the brain, especially if a person is standing or sitting up, because the heart is working against gravity. That decreased blood flow can cause a person to lose consciousness. Then, when a person faints, he or she falls down, and most of the time, blood flow to the brain is immediately restored, at which point the person quickly regains consciousness.

We were relieved to know it wasn't a serious condition in and of itself. But it definitely needed to be controlled. So what was the trigger that caused that response in his vagus nerve?

For some, it's the sight of blood. Trauma, hunger, hypertension, exhaustion, heat stroke, and dehydration are other common causes.

Dad's were stress and hunger. Once he knew the triggers, the treatment for his condition was simple: he had to learn to avoid stress and hunger. Perhaps more importantly, he had to know the warning signs of a fainting spell. When he felt one coming on, getting himself in a position where his head was lower than his heart would prevent the loss of consciousness.

Thankfully, that diagnosis was spot-on. He's never had another Sunday morning fainting spell. But in 1993, we knew eventually something would have to give in regards to his preaching schedule and the amount of stress the church was creating for him.

I'm not sure why I wasn't at North church the night its closing was announced. I've obsessed over where I was that night, and the only thing I can come up with is that I was keeping the baby nursery at the South church that evening, like I had done every Sunday night since its opening.

Beau's wife, Kim, was there. She stood with Mom, holding onto her arm, while Beau went to find Dad. "I've blocked out what she said, though. Can't remember a thing," Kim says, but this is what she took away from the evening: "It sounds dumb now, but that awful night was when I decided I was only having two kids so that I would have an arm for each one in a situation like that."

Truthfully, I think it was God's providence that I wasn't there to see people going after my mom and dad. I'm a bit protective of people I love, and I have a history of decimating those who treat my loved ones badly.[63] So I can only imagine how ugly things might have gotten if I'd actually seen my mom crying.

Just as I had not witnessed the verbal attacks, I wasn't aware of the beautiful letters my dad received from church members who were supportive of the move. In researching this book, I found many of those letters, and I was touched by their words.

---

63 There's a taxi driver in Cozumel, Mexico, who will readily attest to this. And a ticket agent at Walt Disney World.

One South church member wrote, "I was raised in a church in Michigan, and I think the location I grew up in was their third move. They are currently in the process of a fourth move. People sometimes lose sight of the fact that the 'church' is not a building but a congregation of *people*."

I'm not sure the emotional trauma for my dad was as great as the earlier church split had been, but I do believe it was for my mother. And while I don't think any of us – my parents, my brother, my sister, or I – realized it at the time, I truly believe that this was the beginning of the end for my parents. They had, at that point, been in ministry for over thirty years. And it was around that time that Dad asked Beau to take on more of the pastoral duties at the church.

I Shall Not Be Moved

I shall not be, I shall not be moved
Just like a tree that's planted by the water
I shall not be moved[64]

In 1995, once construction on the classroom building had begun, Buford asked Len McWilliams, the school principal, to plan for the school's expansion at the South campus. A trailer boasting a large "Coming Soon!" sign was placed on the site, and Len kept a staff member there to give out information and provide tours to potential students and their families.

Enrollment didn't progress as they had hoped. In the summer of 1996, not long after the decision had been made to move everything to Henry County, and just as the new classroom building was nearing completion, Len told Buford that because the majority of his school families preferred the Clayton County campus, he needed to keep it open. To do so, he had to apply for separate non-profit federal tax identification for the school (the school had, for years, been under the church's charter). Buford approved his request. With just weeks to go before the 1996-97 school year was to begin, Len delivered the message that he had procured the new tax ID and that the school was now under his direction. In addition, he announced that the school's name would change to Community Christian Academy, and it would remain at the Reynolds Road location. He would not participate in the move to Stockbridge. Buford was surprised and disappointed at Len's seeming duplicity, yet he decided not to fight him for the school, mostly because the church would no longer have a presence in Clayton County.

Then Len announced that he believed the church should give Community Christian Academy (the North school) the Reynolds Road facilities. Buford laughed at the idea. "We needed that money. It was twenty-plus years of blood, sweat, and tears. We couldn't just *give* it away," he says.

Len took his appeal to the Board of Elders, who at first seemed stunned by the request. Then they, too, turned him down.

The Reynolds Road property was not listed with a real estate agent, but Buford put out the word that the property was for sale. Within a matter of weeks, he had two offers from two different churches. Len balked at both offers, saying he couldn't keep the school in operation if the buildings were sold to either of those churches.[65] Buford called a friend named Tommy Aman, who was pastor of Rock Springs Baptist Church in nearby Conley, and asked if Rock Springs would be interested in the property, adding that they would have immediate rental income from the Christian school. Aman considered the offer for a few weeks before calling to say Rock Springs had decided to purchase the property.[66] On September 22, 1996, in a specially-called meeting, the Board of Elders voted to sell the property to Rock Springs Baptist Church.

---

[65] One of the churches was New Birth Missionary Baptist Church, which was pastored by Eddie Long.

[66] The actual price paid by Rock Springs was nearly $500,000 less than the other two churches had offered, and Community Bible had to finance the deal.

I Shall Not Be Moved

In a letter addressed to the Elders that was published in the September 23 issue of the church newsletter, Len McWilliams wrote

Thank you for the many sacrifices on behalf of the school throughout the years and for the opportunity to exhaust every avenue to purchase. The efforts by Geoff Marott and Keith Glore this week have been beyond the call of duty and are greatly appreciated. At this time we feel the financial arrangements cannot be met with satisfactory results for both parties. Being aware of the other proposals before the church, any goodwill that might be afforded the school will be served best by positive response to the proposal by Rock Springs Baptist Church.

Around the same time, small church named Tabernacle of Faith Christian Church made an offer to buy the Powerplay building on Reynolds Road. Community financed both deals for over a year before finally helping both churches secure financing through First State Bank in Stockbridge. The remaining sixteen or so acres of the Reynolds Road property was purchased by a land conservation group that deeded it back to Reynolds Nature Preserve. That sales price was more than double what the church had paid for it in 1982.

Beau and Jack both say that moving day in September 1996 was tense. "Dad was pointing at things and saying, 'This goes with us, this goes,' and Len was there making sure we didn't take anything we shouldn't," Beau says of trying to sort out what belonged to the church and what belonged to the school. Volunteers showed up with trucks and trailers to help the staff members pack up and haul everything to the Jodeco campus.

Much of the crowd who voiced opposition to the church's move left after Rock Springs purchased the Reynolds Road facilities.

But some stayed and have been very happy under Tommy Aman's pastorate. Art and Becky Melton, members since the earliest days of the church (Becky was the church's first pianist) were one of those couples. Having lived in Morrow for many years, they chose to give Rock Springs a try, and they are still happily worshipping there today.

For many years, a portrait of Dad hung in the church auditorium's vestibule at the big building on Reynolds Road. Ken Webb, a member who was an award-winning photographer, had taken it, and it was a nice likeness, although people always joked that like the *Mona Lisa*, his eyes followed you.

The portrait made it onto someone's truck on moving day in the fall of 1996, but then it disappeared. Apparently, it collected dust in the attic of the Stockbridge auditorium building for a few years before a maintenance man discovered it in the church dumpster and pulled it out.[67]

In the summer of 2003, my husband and I walked into the bedroom of our Destin, Florida, condo for a couple weeks' vacation. I dropped my suitcase onto the floor of the closet, then walked into the master bathroom and switched on the light. I got the shock of a lifetime – that portrait of Dad was hanging over our garden tub. My sister, Holly, and her husband had used the condo weeks before and replaced a generic decorator-grade painting with the portrait, obviously something of much greater sentimental value.

A few months later, Beau helped me smuggle "the Buford" into Holly's house to hang it over their master bed.

---

67 Buford is the alleged culprit, but no one has been able to prove that he put the portrait in the dumpster.

I Shall Not Be Moved

At that point, it was Beau's turn to be startled by what was now our version of the world-travelling Garden Gnome. Holly and I waited for nearly a year for the perfect opportunity, and Beau handed it to us on a silver platter. He began a sermon series titled "The Monsters in Your Closet" that dealt with attitudes and emotions that are spiritually debilitating – greed, lust, anger, etc. Jeremy Cabe, who constructed elaborate sets for Beau's sermon series, had built a "closet" on the stage. Every week, Beau would walk over to that closet and fling open the door to reveal a cartoonish lurking "monster," a terrific visual illustration of what we need to clean out of our emotional closets. One Sunday morning, Holly and I practically twisted Jeremy's arm (he was understandably nervous about irritating the boss!) to get him to hide the portrait of Dad in the closet at an angle that only Beau could see when he opened the door.

We sat close to the front that morning so that we could see Beau's face when he opened the door. The moment arrived. He walked over and swung open the closet to reveal the Greed monster, and . . . nothing happened. His expression never changed, and he went right on preaching.

Holly and I approached him after the service, demanding to know how he'd covered it so well. He looked at us like we were crazy, then walked over and looked inside the closet. He burst out laughing. It was in there, but he just hadn't seen it. All he said was, "I was wondering why you two were sitting so close to the front today."

"The Buford" has made its rounds over the years, once showing up as part of the elaborate Christmas decorations outside my sister's home. It even made an appearance at Mom and Dad's Fiftieth Wedding Anniversary celebration in August of 2013.

Count Your Blessings

Count your many blessings --
name them one by one,
And it will surprise you what the Lord has done[68]

Sunday, September 8, 1997, was Reunification Sunday. The church began preparations for the day months in advance by holding another telephone campaign, this one known at Telefriend, during which thousands of Henry County residents were contacted by telephone and invited to church. "Ninety percent of all the people who come to church and get involved do it because someone invited them," Buford says, and to that end, church members were encouraged to invite their unchurched friends to a new service that was planned for that day. Dubbed the "outreach" service, it would meet during the 9:30 worship hour. The dress would be casual, and the music "geared toward the tastes of a younger crowd," according to a church newsletter dated July 15, 1996.

The outreach service was something that Buford and Beau had been working on for over a year.

In July 1995, Brad and Jill Ellis visited Community Bible Church's South campus. The young couple had recently moved into a new house less than a mile from the church. Tall and thin,

---

68 Written by Johnson Oatman, Jr.

with his prematurely silver hair pulled into a ponytail, Brad looked like a musician.[69] In fact, he was a songwriter who had been in several Christian bands during the late seventies and early eighties, but the experience had been so negative that he had vowed never to sing or play in front of a church again. "Every time we visited a church, after about a month they would find out my background and ask me to sing, and I'd leave because I was done. I'd grown up in the church, and I knew Jesus. Me and Jesus were good," he says, admitting that they were there solely to get their children "grounded in church."

They went to a Sunday school class and immediately made some friends. Brad says, "We joined the church off of Sunday school and Jack's preaching because Buford was on vacation for the first few weeks we were here." They sat on the back row, preferring to be left alone, mostly because Brad didn't want anyone asking him to help with the music. They watched carefully how services were conducted and how the church was run because, in Brad's words, "We were leery of the family connection between the pastor (Buford) and the youth pastor (Beau) because of our background" during the early 1980s in a church he says was "very much like a cult."

One morning, Buford approached Brad to say that he knew his background and that the church was looking to start a new kind of worship service with more contemporary Christian music. "Usually that sent me running," Brad says. Buford asked him to advise them on how to build and structure the service and its music. "I told him I would help them get it started, but I would

---

69 Mike Smith, an early member of the South church, says that the first time he saw Brad Ellis sitting on the back row during the morning service, he thought *one of the Oak Ridge Boys is here.*

never be a part of it. I would never participate, but I could tell them what not to do."

Not long after that, Beau invited Brad to go with him and Jack to visit several contemporary services in the Atlanta area to get an idea of what they wanted for the new service at Community. They found what they were looking for at Orange Hill Church in Austell. Sonny Lallerstedt, a former member of the Christian bands Dove and the Pat Terry Group, was the worship leader. "I remember sitting in that service and thinking, *I could do this*," Brad says. "I could feel what Sonny was doing and the way they ran their music, and I thought it was doable." Brad and Beau got back into the church van after the service, and Beau asked Brad what he thought. "That's your pattern right there. This is good, and it will work," he told Beau.

But when Beau looked at him and asked who could be their worship leader, Brad said, "I can't tell you that. But I don't like to sing, and I don't play piano. I'm not gonna do it."

A few weeks later, Beau introduced Brad to a new couple who were visiting the church, Glenn and Cindy Hall. "You're a song-writer, and you're a songwriter. I just thought you two should meet," he said to both men. He handed Brad a tape of Glenn's music and said, "Check this out."

Brad says he went home, listened to the tape, and thought yeah, *I can feel where this guy is at.*

Then, early in the summer of 1996, Brad says, Beau called him. "Hey, we're having a meeting this Friday night for anyone inter-ested in helping build this new service." When Brad promised to be at the meeting, Beau said, "Do you think you could open the meeting for us with a song?"

"I'm not gonna do it, Beau. I'm not gonna sing," was the response.

Glenn Hall sang that night. And while he sat in the audience listening to Glenn's original song, Brad says he thought, *we are on the same vibe here.*

After the service, the two stood at the auditorium's grand piano playing a game of what Brad calls "Check This Out," singing for one another different songs they were in the process of writing. "I remember looking over my shoulder and seeing Beau and Jack and a couple of other people watching us and smiling, so I looked at Glenn and said, 'What do you think? Can we do this?'"

By the end of the evening, a couple of other people had committed to help start the band. And just like Buford Adams told his original congregation nearly thirty years before, Brad said, "I'll help get it started. I'll get you going, and then I'm done."

The original group of four – Brad, Glenn, Chris Davis, and Tom Rich[70] – began rehearsing to be ready for the debut of the "outreach" service on September 8, 1996.

They weren't the only ones preparing for that Sunday. South church choir and orchestra members began driving between churches on Sunday mornings to fill spots left empty in Clayton County by those upset over its closing. A group of volunteers were recruited to plan a dinner on the grounds following the September 8 services. And by starting the kind of service that not many people had ever seen, Beau put himself in the hot seat. Would people accept the new, more casual style of worship? Would they be okay with him sitting on a stool rather than standing behind a pulpit to preach? And would they accept him? He'd grown up in the church, and to be sure, he was loved at Community. But in addition to being a new lead pastor in a church service, he was also bringing big change to an established place. Inherent in that kind of change is the chance of being roundly rejected. Remembering those early

---

70 The band was later named "Second Chance."

days of the outreach service, Beau says, "You would have thought we were killing babies when we decided to get rid of the organ."

Buford began preparing the membership for the new service by explaining that the kind of service people were used to wasn't going away. The traditional service would stay in its regular time slot. But he told the membership that they were "beginning the new service because the younger generations are sometimes turned off to church tradition." Citing the words of the Apostle Paul, "I have become all things to all people so that by all possible means I might save some,"[71] he said those words should become the church's theme as it moved into the 21st century because that attitude is part of becoming a mature Christian.

All that planning paid off. Reunification Sunday was a resounding success. The worship service attendance numbers reported for Sunday, March 17, the morning of the announcement that the two churches would combine on September 8, were 602 for the North campus and 739 for South (1,341 combined). On September 8, 1996, the numbers were 773 for the new outreach service and 947 for the 11 o'clock traditional service (1,720 combined). During the dinner on the grounds that followed the morning services, Buford and Beau must have breathed a sigh of relief. Community Bible Church North and South was now just Community Bible Church, and it had weathered the storm.

The attendance numbers in the traditional service held steady throughout the fall and winter, while the new service, now called the "contemporary" service, dropped a bit. But on Easter Sunday, it became apparent to everyone involved (and most likely, to everyone at Community Bible Church that morning) that they were onto

---

71 I Corinthians 9:22 (NIV). Incidentally, it was this same verse the teenagers used in convincing the Elders to approve the Trail of Terror in the early 1980s.

something big. The church had sent out another mailing to the entire county with the caption "Which Came First, Easter or the Egg?" The inside copy read, "On Easter Sunday, April 4, Community Bible Church has something for everyone! Choose which worship service you'd like to attend – 8:30, 9:30, or 11:00 – and then plan for our Easter egg hunt. We know the 'Which Came First' answer requires a little theological nitpicking, but this Easter Sunday at Community Bible Church, the answer depends on which service you attend!" The church hadn't hosted an Easter egg hunt in years, but that old tried and true formula of bringing in the Easter Bunny (this time by fire truck, not helicopter), worked just as magically as it had nearly a quarter of a century earlier, in 1973.

That morning, the 8:30 service that was added just for Easter Sunday was large enough that it stuck, meaning Buford was once again preaching twice on Sunday mornings. At the start of the contemporary service, Brad Ellis says he looked up from the keyboard and saw people crowding the foyer waiting to be seated. "It was this huge feeling of *what have we done? What have we created? That was the day we knew that this was going to work.*"

One other monumental thing happened on that Easter Sunday -- the contemporary service's attendance was larger than that of the traditional service. And that would continue to be true until the present day. When asked what he believes is the key to the contemporary service's success, Brad Ellis didn't hesitate: "Honesty. There's no pretense from anyone on that stage. We're just who we are." He laughed and added, "We've done all kinds of things. I even sang Jimmy Buffett from the pulpit! But I think the attraction is that everyone on that stage is real."[72]

---

72 To promote the "Recovery" series of messages, the church sent out a mailer quoting a line from "A Pirate Looks at 40." Brad changed two words when he sang the song during morning worship service.

I Am Loved at Community Bible Church

By the fall of 1999, the church offered four Sunday morning worship services. The "High Church" service, led by Buford, met at 8:30 in the newly constructed Chapel. A liturgical service with Scripture readings, communion, and organ music, it was an intimate service for those who preferred a formal style of worship. Then at 11:00, he led another service in the Chapel with old-fashioned hymns in what was called a "Traditional" service. Beau led both services in the auditorium – the 9:30 Contemporary for those preferring music by Second Chance, and an 11:00 service that was a blend of the band and its newer Christian music accompanied by the full choir and orchestra.

As a family, we always knew it was more a matter of when than if there would be a mishap involving Dad's lapel microphone. I guess it's not surprising that it happened when he was once again preaching two services.

The lavalier microphone was invented in the late 1950s and first used nationally during television broadcasts of the 1960 Republican and Democratic conventions. The device was named after a particular pendant worn by the Duchess de la Valierre, a mistress of Louis XIV, because it is most often clipped at the neckline.

The church purchased its first lavalier mic in the mid-1970s, allowing the pastoral staff to roam the stage while speaking. Dad loved his and lamented the loss of the church's first one when all hell broke loose during the church's first formal baptism service. The ability to forget about speaking directly into the microphone and the freedom from being confined to a two-foot square during a forty-five minute message seemed to add a new vigor to his sermons.[73]

But with great freedom comes great responsibility.

Unfortunately, that lapel mic was so unobtrusive that one could easily forget it was attached or that it was turned on. For example, during a five-year-old-kindergarten graduation program a few years ago, as the children were filing in and filling up the stage, the young emcee, wearing a dark suit and a lavalier mic, leaned over to the boy next to him and, not knowing he was "on," whispered, "This is BULLSHIT!"

Needless to say, Dad was completely aware of the dangers of having the equivalent of three megaphones four inches from his face. And for nearly twenty years, he successfully avoided doing what we once saw depicted in a church cartoon: A pastor leans over to his associate pastor following a lovely operatic version of "O Holy Night" and whispers, "The fat lady has sung. Can we just go home?"

But early one Sunday before church, as the choir and orchestra were rehearsing for the morning service at the South campus, the unthinkable happened. Over the speakers came a tinkling sound followed by the unmistakable "whoosh" of a flushing toilet. Dad emerged from the restroom to hear uproarious laughter coming from the auditorium, and he immediately realized he was "on."

Thankfully, he had remembered to wash his hands.

---

73 It also gave a music teacher at the Christian school the freedom to make his way down the aisle dressed in a red, white, and blue vest singing Neil Diamond's "We're Coming to America" backed by sixty elementary-school children.

God Leads Us Along

Some through the waters, some through the flood,
Some through the fire, but all through the blood;
Some through great sorrow, but God gives a song,
In the night season and all the day long.[74]

The splitting off of the school from the church left a huge hole in the ministry that Buford didn't have the time or the energy to fix. In the spring of 1996, he got a call from a pastor friend in South Florida, Jimmy Sheffield, who was originally from Atlanta and had been one of the Youth Ranch kids in the late 1960s.[75] Jimmy was leaving South Florida and the pastorate, and he asked for Buford's advice on what he should do next.

Under Jimmy's leadership, Florida Bible Church had built an impressive Christian school, so Buford eventually invited him to move to Stockbridge and help start a school. Within a year, in the same location where Len McWilliams had tried twice and failed, Jimmy and his wife, Tricia, launched a preschool, kindergarten,

---

74 Words and music by George A. Young

75 Jimmy's step-father was George Pace, the man who had helped Buford find, refurbish, and operate the church's first printing press. Mr. Pace and his wife, Liddie, Jimmy's mother, were faithful church members for many years.

and elementary school that was soon a thriving and profitable part of Community.

The church began a new building fund campaign in 1997 that would be the largest in its history in terms of added space (and, therefore, cost). Called Building the Best, the campaign sought to raise $3.5 million for a gymnasium, more classroom space, a chapel, and an atrium that would connect all of the structures and serve as a central gathering spot.

First State Bank in Stockbridge, eager for the church's business, agreed to finance the two loans the church was carrying following the sale of its properties to Rock Springs Baptist and Tabernacle of Faith Christian Church if they could also finance the new project. The payout from those loans plus the profit of the undeveloped Reynolds Road land helped toward the financing of the project, and an anonymous donor offered to match dollar for dollar anything given up to $70,000. That project was completed in the summer of 1998.

The added space allowed the church to expand the Children's Ministry, which was crucial for a church located in a neighborhood full of young families. The church began offering Trunk 'n Treat on Halloween, with church members dressing up and giving out candy in the church parking lot from the trunks of their decorated cars. No one knows how many Skittles have been handed out over the years, but thousands of Henry County residents show up for Trunk 'n Treat every Halloween.

One Sunday evening, the church brought in a hot air balloon to give kids rides. The plan was to keep the balloon tethered, put a few kids in the basket at a time, and simply let it float into the air about fifty feet high before pulling it back down. Holly Adams, who was the Children's Minister at the time, says, "The balloon was inflated, and we were all ready to go when a thunderstorm came roaring through. It was a hot summer evening, and the storm came in pretty fast. The guy who owned the balloon was afraid that it was going to be torn up, so he was working frantically to get it down. In the process, the balloon draped itself over a light pole. The pole popped the balloon and was sticking through it. Then the storm was on us. It was pouring down rain and lightning was flashing. The guy was desperate to get his balloon off of the light pole. Chip Flanegan put an aluminum ladder against the light pole and climbed it during the storm to rescue the balloon."[76]

Community Christian School opened its doors in the fall of 1997, offering Kindergarten for ages three to five. The next year, grades one through three were added. In its third year of operations, CCS offered Kindergarten through sixth grades, and it also added several new classes in order to accommodate more students in the lower grades. In addition, they began adding one new grade each year at the top so that Community Christian School would celebrate its first graduating class in 2006.

Every once in a while, God sends a reminder that His hand is on the ministry. In 2012, a woman parking her Jeep Liberty in a spot next to the preschool building blacked out. Her car jumped the curb and crashed into a classroom positioned at the front of the building. Had children been in the room at the time of the crash, the story could have been a tragic one. But that room was empty on that particular day because there was a leak in the ceiling, and its denizens had been moved to another room while the leak was being repaired. No one, not even the woman driving the car, was injured.

---

[76] Chip is another original Youth Ranch teenager who is still a church member.

God Leads Us Along

In the spring of 2014, school enrollment stood at 838, with a faculty and staff of just over 200. The school is dually accredited through the Southern Association of Colleges and Schools (SACS) and SAIS. Community's high school is graduating students who score fifty points higher than the Georgia average on the SAT, and its students graduate with 28 credit hours versus the state-required 23. The school offers AP classes and dual enrollment through Truett McConnell College. Graduates have been accepted at over sixty colleges and universities, including Georgia Institute of Technology, Emory University, St. Johns University, the University of Georgia, the University of Hawaii, and the University of Virginia.

Tricia Sheffield once told me a story that I think perfectly defines the experience of teaching preschoolers. A little four-year-old boy was sent to her office for misbehaving. The boy seemed to listen intently as she spoke of how important it was for him to respect his teacher and do what she said. He looked her right in the eyes the whole time she was talking. When she finished, she asked the little guy if he understood what she'd said. Without breaking eye contact, he leaned forward and said, "You don't got no eyebrows!"

I was one of the students enrolled at Clayton Christian School when its doors opened in the fall of 1973, and my daughters were students on the first day of classes at the brand new Community Christian School in 1998. My oldest child, Morgan, was in the third grade during Community Christian's inaugural year. Second and third grades were in the same classroom, learning under the expert eye of Mrs. Carolyn Vickrey. There were fewer than ten in that class, and Morgan was the only girl.

I'm not sure, though, that my girl ever loved CCS like I did. In fact, she even said as much. She was eight, and one morning on the way to school, she flipped down the front passenger seat visor to check her reflection in the mirror. Rather than fussing with her hair as I expected, she turned her head from side to side and uttered a quick, guttural, "Uggh!" followed by, "I HATE school!"

I opened my mouth to say, "What's so bad about school?"

But before I could ask, she blurted out the reason. "The fluorescent lighting makes me look horrible."

Her little sister, Lauren, was in Mrs. Stauffer's kindergarten that first year. At the end of the year, Mrs. Stauffer asked every child in the class to tell her the recipe for their favorite food. She copied every recipe and created a "cookbook" for the parents.

Lauren didn't hesitate when asked what was her favorite food. It was the chicken biscuit. Her recipe began with killing a chicken, plucking the feathers, and cutting it into pieces the right size for a chicken biscuit before breading it and then cooking it (my girl knew her stuff!). When she began explaining how to make a biscuit, Mrs. Stauffer interrupted and said, "Let's hurry this up, Lauren."

Lauren looked at her, shrugged, and said, "Or you could just go to Truett's."

Truett's was a fairly new restaurant when Lauren recommended it in her recipe. Opened in Morrow, Georgia, in 1995 as Chick-Fil-A's tribute to Truett Cathy's 50th Anniversary in the restaurant business, it had become a favorite place for our family. My dad sent a copy of the cookbook to Mr. Cathy along with a letter explaining the background of the "recipe." A couple of days later, Lauren received an autographed copy of his book along with a couple of free chicken biscuit coupons and his note of thanks for sending new customers to his restaurant.

God Leads Us Along

The school was very important to my family for many years. All three of my children were enrolled there through the eighth grade before going on to graduate from public high schools. They have done well academically, and I credit the excellent foundation they received at Community.

But my gratitude to the school goes much deeper than what it did for my own kids because there's a group of men scattered around the world whose lives were changed because of Community Christian School.

In 2004, my husband introduced Jimmy Sheffield to one of our neighbors, a man named Linzy Davis. Linzy was a member of Nike's national high school basketball board and the coach of the United States U-18 national basketball team. Linzy wanted to bring a group of ten or twelve elite international basketball players into the school to be educated. The idea was to give these boys a chance at a college education because the United States is the only country in the world that awards college scholarships for athletics. Linzy's international travel with the American team gave him the opportunity to see some of the best junior players in the world. He persuaded the school to let him screen the players and choose not only the best athletes but, more importantly, those who could be successful in the school and would make the most of the opportunity they had been given. The school jumped at the opportunity, and four new students -- one from Canada, one from Nigeria, one from Malawi, and one from Lithuania – enrolled in the fall of 2003.

One year later, Beau called to tell me that the program was being shut down. "Why are you ending it?" I asked. He explained that Jimmy Sheffield had resigned as school administrator, and his successor was frustrated by the amount of his time the program required. In addition, the program had cost the school nearly $40,000 the previous year. Closing the program meant that the international students, including six new ones who had just arrived, would be sent back to their respective countries.

With no hesitation, I said, "I'll run the program."

Very quickly, my brother said, "It's yours."

Two days later, I found myself in a conference room with the new school administrator, the school principal, the athletic director, Linzy, and a woman named Joy Clemons, who had named herself my assistant the minute she heard that I had volunteered to oversee the program.

The meeting lasted nearly two hours, with the school administrator venting his frustrations over finances and his concerns over how we planned to house the five new boys who had just arrived. As Joy furiously took notes, I naively promised to address all the administrator's concerns immediately.

The next afternoon, Joy and I strolled into the gym at 3:15, when basketball practice was scheduled to start, so that I could meet the new players. Standing at the free throw line practicing his shots was the biggest kid I had ever seen in my life. He was built more like a defensive lineman for the Green Bay Packers than a basketball player -- massive shoulders and a huge torso supported by the biggest legs I'd ever seen on a human being; his calves looked like the trunks of an average-sized cherry tree. He had blond hair and wore a huge grin on his face.

"That's Petras," Joy said. "He's from Lithuania."

None of the coaches were in the gym, and it was time to start practice. I called to Solomon, one of the players from the previous year and this year's team captain, and told him to start warm-ups. While the rest of the team began stretching, the big blonde boy walked over to me and said in a voice that can only be described as slightly Baltic, a little Russian-sounding, and kind of ghetto, "Can you tape up my hand?"

I looked at his hand. He had a deep gash about three inches long across his palm. "What happened?"

"I cut it opening a can of applesauce."

It was confirmation that the boys' living situation was as bad as the school administrator had said.

"You're not going to practice with your hand like that, are you?" I said.

"I be all right."

I went home that evening and told my husband we would soon be housing a student from another country, knowing that the only way I could persuade other families to house an international student was to lead by example. Petras moved into our house a month later. My kids immediately loved their new big brother.

Within a few weeks, Joy and I had secured host families for all of the boys who had been living in the "dorm," a house across the street from the church that had been purchased with the intention of tearing down in order to build new ball fields.

During the next two school years, we hosted boys from Poland, Angola, France, Nigeria, Lithuania, Ivory Coast, Canada, and the Canary Islands. A few did not even speak English when they came to the school.

At the beginning of the 2005-06 school year, the high school English teacher, a nice enough woman who had her hands full with the school's regular students, put her foot down one day and refused to give extra help to the international students. I was frantic. Without a sympathetic English teacher, the boys who were not native English speakers would be in serious trouble. And really, they needed a course focused on helping them pass the SAT and preparing them for freshman English — assuming they actually made it to college.

I went to the school administrator to voice my concerns, and he said, "You're so concerned about their English. Why don't you teach it?"

"Okay. I will." I had a degree in English, after all.

And then he said, "Oh, and we have a young lady from South Korea who is an exchange student with one of our school families. She'll be in your class, too."

It's one thing to teach English. But teaching English as a Second Language to eight young men and one girl -- all from different countries and cultures -- when I'd never taught before was another. I was scared.

I looked around the room the very first day of my English as a Second Language Class and wondered what I'd gotten myself into. My class was comprised of three Polish guys — Jakub, Krzysztof, and Aleks — Solomon from Nigeria, Baptiste from France, Petras from Lithuania, Ousmane from Ivory Coast, the little South Korean girl named Noah, and C.J., a kid from Albany, Georgia, who was in my class because he had no hope of passing regular English. The average height of my students would have been around 6'8", but little Noah barely hit 5 feet, bringing the average down considerably.

To begin the class, I passed out books. First was Phil Jackson's *Sacred Hoops*. Now, at the time, I was not an expert teacher. This was my first day in the classroom, and I'd been given no curriculum. In fact, until I devised my own curriculum, I'm not sure one existed that focused on teaching teenagers from different continents enough English to pass the SAT in six months. The one thing I knew for certain was that they had to read to be successful. To get them to read, I had to find books that interested them. At the time, Phil Jackson had coached his teams to nine NBA titles,[77] more than any coach in history, and he was Michael Jordan's coach during the years the Chicago Bulls dominated the NBA. I was pretty sure he could keep those guys' attention.

I handed out the spelling and vocabulary books, explaining that since we needed to cram as many English words as we could into their brains before the SAT, they would be required to write five sentences, each using a new vocabulary word correctly, every night as part of their homework.

The next day, my students arrived for class and dutifully turned in their vocabulary assignments. That evening, I checked over them for accuracy, and when I got to Solomon's, I laughed out loud. The vocabulary word was "profane." Solomon, the one his teammates called "preacher" because of his professed devotion to Christianity (and also the one who struggled the most with his English), had written, "It was profane for the soldiers to stable their whores in the church."

He got an A. It was a perfectly correct use of the word "profane."

One of the teams these boys played came from a school named Genesis One in Mendenhall, Mississippi. It's a school that was started in 1977 by an organization called the "Voice of Calvary." The name was later changed to Mendenhall Ministries, and Dolphus Weary – the same man who spoke at Clayton Community Church in the early 1980s -- was their president. Weary has since stepped down from that position, but he remains an active supporter of Mendenhall Ministries.

The program was closed down at the end of the 2005-06 school year, when the majority of the boys graduated. The two who were still in high school, Olu Ashalou and Junior Cadougan, transferred

---

77 1991, 1992, 1993 Chicago Bulls, and 1996, 1997, 1998, 1999, 2001, and 2002 Los Angeles Lakers

to a Christian school in Houston that had an elite basketball team, and they went on to have successful college careers.[78] Every one of those boys developed close relationships with their host families. They're now scattered around the world, some back in their native countries and some playing professional basketball in Europe and South America, but they still call "home" to check in.

I'll forever be proud of what CCS did for those boys. While they were all terrific athletes, and some are still playing professionally in other countries, none made it to the big money of the NBA. However, most of them would never have even gone to college if it hadn't been for Community Christian School.

At the end of his high school graduation ceremony, Petras handed me a card. The loud, outspoken boy who was fluent in five languages had simply written, "Ms. Sandi, I will never forget this."

---

[78] Junior Cadougan was the starting point guard for Marquette during his last three years of college. While he was there, the team made two Sweet Sixteen appearances, and in 2012, they were ranked in the AP and *USA Today*/Coach's Poll Top Ten.

Rock of Ages

Rock of Ages, cleft for me,
Let me hide myself in thee.[79]

Members were being added to the church so quickly Buford and Beau began to fear that people new to the church were unfamiliar with its history and its purpose. They began holding a membership class called Community 101 that eventually became a requirement for membership at Community. The class, taught by Buford, Beau, and Jack, detailed the church's history, beginning with the Atlanta Youth Ranch and its mission to evangelize teenagers. It pointed out that the church's primary focus hadn't changed over the years. It explained the church's fundamental beliefs and how it is governed. The class culminated in a call for new members to volunteer in some capacity, whether it be teaching Sunday school, holding babies in the nursery, working with the youth ministry, directing traffic in the church parking lot, or selling coffee between services in the church atrium's Holy Grounds coffee bar. The church's pastoral staff had, for a long time, believed that the key to a new member's happiness rested in how quickly he or she began developing relationships in the church. Getting new members into a small group – a more intimate setting such as Sunday school or a Bible study – helped

79 Words by Augustus M. Toplady

them develop friendships in the church, and that was important. But volunteering developed relationships *and* immediately made people feel useful and needed. "Every member a minister" was the theme, the idea being that when we pitch in and help, we're less likely to sit back and criticize.

During a membership class sometime in 2001, Buford was waxing eloquent on the need to get involved when a man in the back raised his hand. Buford acknowledged the man and asked if he had a question.

"Who are you?" the man said.

It was a new century, and the contemporary service, with its casual style, modern music, and Beau's informal, conversational approach to preaching, was more appealing to the younger families walking through the doors every Sunday. Community was reaching a new generation. The Greatest Generation and their Baby Boomer sons and daughters had magnificently shouldered the responsibilities of the church through the years, but now it was time for the Generation Xers and the Millennials to carry the torch. Change had come, and to their credit, neither Buford nor Beau resisted it.

Within a year of its beginning, the contemporary service had outgrown the traditional services at Community. And by 2001, even the 11:00 auditorium service, the one billed as a blend of the contemporary and traditional styles of worship, had shifted to contemporary. Realizing that Beau's style of preaching was part of the draw, Buford began making plans for retiring and leaving the church in the hands of his son. Thirty-two years after he agreed to lead the fledgling church until a permanent pastor could be found, he found that guy.

In 2002, Buford and Babs sold their house in McDonough, Georgia, and moved to a neighborhood of old Florida cottage-style homes very close to the beach in St. Augustine, Florida. For the first few years, they drove back to Atlanta frequently to be at church on Sunday mornings, and Buford filled in for Beau when he was on vacation.

Then something happened that prompted Beau to begin using the other pastors on staff to cover his vacations. The story is better told in Buford's words:

"After I retired, Beau asked me to speak for him one week while he was on vacation. I'm not sure if I was just not interested in speaking or if I was feeling rebellious,[80] but that Sunday morning I wore a Jimmy Buffett shirt with Margaritaville logos[81] all over it, and I ended the sermon by telling a joke that went something like this:

Two good ol' boys from Alabama were seated at a restaurant having lunch when the lady at the table next to them began to choke on her food. One of them looked at the other and asked should they help her. They got up, and one picked her up by her ankles and held her upside down while the other whacked her on the rear end. It startled her so much that she coughed, and it dislodged the food stuck in her throat. They righted her and helped her get seated back at the table. Then one looked at the other and said, "you know, that hiney-lick maneuver works every time, don't it?

"I thought it was funny," Buford says, "but a kind of nervous laughter went through the audience. Babs was mortified, and the next morning, the church receptionist, Carole McDonald, answered several phone calls from people who thought the joke was offensive.

---

80 Or perhaps it was his most "contemporary" shirt?
81 In other words, it was covered in margarita glasses

"About two weeks later, I was playing golf with Carole's husband, Hugh. At one particular tee box, there was a flock of Canadian geese off to the side. I teed my ball up and swung as hard as I could and managed to shank the ball 100 degrees to the right. It hit one of the geese right in the rear – a perfect shot. Hugh and I doubled over with laughter."

Not long after that, the doorbell rang at their home in Florida, and the postman had Buford sign for a registered letter. It looked like a legal document from an organization called POOFF -- Protectors of our Feathered Friends. It read, "To the above named defendant: You are hereby summoned to appear and defend in this action which is hereby served upon you and answer. You are being charged with the unlawful rear attack upon a defenseless goose and implantation of a foreign object into the posterior of said goose. If you fail to appear, a judgment of default will be placed against you for the relief."

The document was signed by "Margaret Hineylick."

The incident cemented Buford's retirement. He now preaches one sermon a year – an Easter sunrise service on the beach in St. Augustine – and conducts the occasional beachside wedding and funeral. He was once even called upon to pray over his next-door neighbors who were severely hung over after a raucous party the night before. But to his great relief, he is no longer asked to fill in for Beau.

Several months before my dad retired, my family got to church a few minutes late one Sunday morning, and the only seats available were on the balcony. I remember sitting there looking out over the crowd and thinking that the church had outgrown my abilities as its Publications Director. After debating for a few weeks, I resigned from the job I'd had for nearly fifteen years, the only job I'd had as an adult. It was a tough decision, but I reasoned that if I were to continue in the job, I needed to upgrade my page layout skills. Advances in graphic design software had left me in the page design Dark Ages. I had taught myself Photoshop and QuarkXPress, but I was hardly an expert in using them. In addition, the church had gotten to the point where it likely needed someone full-time for the position. Finally, I was forced to acknowledge that what I really wanted to do was write. I have always believed I was put on this planet to write books, and it was time for me to either put up or shut up.

It's probably a good thing I stepped down when I did. Although I'm a master at deciphering my dad's handwriting, I've never been able to read my brother's, so the weekly sermon notes might have turned out terribly wrong.

It's funny what you remember a decade after you leave a job. In researching for this book, I picked through boxes of old files, and when I came to a fat file labeled "Car Count," I had to laugh.

My whole life, being a preacher's kid more or less meant being at church every time the doors were open. I don't recall missing many Sunday services during the years I was growing up, even when we were on vacation and hundreds of miles from home, because on those days, we visited other churches so that Dad could check out the competition.

We would enter a new church, sit down, and observe every single thing about the place – the order of service, how the members greeted visitors, and, of course, the sermon. Once, we were sitting in a pew waiting for a service to start when an older couple waddled up and stared at us before the woman sniffed and said in a loud voice, "NOW where are we going to sit?"

But what I remember most vividly is Sunday mornings and Dad winding his way through church parking lots in vacation towns counting how many cars were in their parking lots.

I never really even cared about what he was doing when he counted cars until I began working at the church as an adult. My first day on the job, I found an 8x11 piece of paper on my desk titled "Car Count." On it were designations for each of the church services, and in each of the blank spaces next to the particular service times, someone had penciled in a number indicating how many cars were in the church parking lot during each service.

My job was to take those numbers and multiply each of them by 2.65 in order to report the number of people in the corresponding worship services. For instance, if the car count said 244 for an 11:00 service, that meant we had 776 in attendance that morning.

Dad had developed the formula over the years by counting actual heads and comparing that number to the number of cars in the church parking lot. Perhaps it was a crude way of counting attendance, but Dad always believed it was better than having someone standing at the back of an auditorium actually counting people. Whether or not it was scientifically accurate, it did provide a consistent baseline for comparing attendance from Sunday to Sunday or from one year to the next, not to mention how our church was doing compared to all those between here and our usual vacation spots in Florida.

Part of my research for this book also involved asking my dad hundreds of questions. When I started this project in the winter of 2012, he wrote down the answers to the first few pages of questions. Then, one day when I stopped by their house, he handed me an old Panasonic RQ-346 portable cassette recorder and said, "It's all on here."

It was the tape recorder he'd used for probably twenty years to dictate his letters and his seminary papers. Nearly every day, he would walk into my office and set a cassette tape on my desk and say, "Here are a few letters," or "Here's the Dear Folks letter." I had a transcribing machine, and I would transcribe and edit his words at the same time. Over the years, I became incredibly adept and fast, and that was a good thing because Dad wrote a lot of letters.

I don't know how many letters I typed over the years, but I do know that not a week went by when I didn't type some sort of Thank You letter for my father. He understood the importance of letting people know that he recognized and appreciated the things done for or given to the church.

What I didn't know then was how good Dad was at dictating. (And I'm not talking about dictating in the sense of being a dictator.) He dictated letters so well that all I really had to do was add appropriate punctuation. In writing for magazines, I've interviewed many people over the years, yet I never realized until I started writing this book that transcribing my dad's words is infinitely easier than it is with anyone else I've ever interviewed.

The old tape recorder was missing the "door" that held the tapes, so I had to hold it carefully upright to keep the cassettes from dropping out. He used old tapes from his collection of sermons, erasing the old sermons as he told new old stories about the church's history. For many years, we kept a library of every single one of his sermons, and I laughed when he handed me a tape dated August 14, 1984 (#1165 in his library) with the sermon title "Forgiveness is Final." He shrugged and said, "No one wants to listen to these anymore."

And that, I think, is when it really hit me. Part of what makes Community great is that we respect and honor our past, but we don't make it so sacred that we're unwilling to change. The nature of life is change, and the road to success is looking unflinchingly into the future and saying, "I'm happy about change because it means I'm still alive. And I'm not afraid because I know God is in control."

'Tis So Sweet

I'm so glad I learned to trust Thee,
Precious Jesus, Savior, Friend;
And I know that Thou art with me,
Wilt be with me to the end[82]

A man came home from work one day to find his three children outside, still wearing their pajamas from the night before. They were playing in the mud, and the dog was lying in the driveway chewing on one of his running shoes. Empty candy bar wrappers and juice boxes were strewn all over the front yard. Picking up his youngest, he asked, "Where's Mommy?"

"We don't know!" the trio chorused.

The front door to the house was open, and he walked in to find an even bigger mess inside. The place looked like it had been ransacked. A lamp was knocked over, and there were muddy footprints everywhere. The television was blaring, and he walked into the kitchen to find it strewn with toys and clothes. Dishes filled the sink, and the table hadn't been cleared from breakfast. The refrigerator was standing open, and there was broken glass on the tile floor in front of the sink.

---

82 Words by Louisa M. R. Stead

Dread rising in his chest, the man ran upstairs looking for his wife, worried that she was ill or, worse, that someone had entered the home and attacked her. As he came down the hallway, he saw water running out of the bathroom. He stopped to turn off the sink's faucet and saw toothpaste smeared all over the bathroom mirror. The whole roll of toilet paper had been unspooled and lay in soggy clumps on the bathroom floor.

He rushed into the master bedroom to find his wife curled up on the bed reading a novel. She looked up at him and smiled, then asked how his day had gone.

Bewildered, he shouted, "What happened here today? Why is this place a wreck?"

Still smiling, his wife said, "You know how every day you come home and ask me what I did all day?"

He nodded, and she continued, "Well, today I didn't."

That joke has been around for years, and it has endured because it speaks to a universal truth, that much of what women do is interior work that is hardly seen, and much less noticed, by society at large.

A good example of this is that for many years, Babs Adams spent one day every week fasting and praying in her little "home office" that doubled as a laundry room. In introducing the Lord's prayer in Matthew 6, Jesus explained how we should pray: "But when you pray, go into your room, close the door and pray to your Father, who is unseen. . . . And when you pray, do not keep on babbling like pagans, for they think they will be heard because of their many words" (Matthew 6:6-7, NIV). Her weekly ritual was Babs' way of obeying the command that prayer should be conducted in private, meaning that it's a personal matter and not something to be flagrantly broadcast in an attempt to showcase one's spirituality. Surely it had a positive effect on both Buford and the church.

Prayer wasn't her only ministry. In the mid-1970s, she was instrumental in building a Ladies' Ministry at the church. Working with a very small budget, volunteers offered classes on topics such as bread making, canning food, and other subjects of interest to women.

And just to be clear, the real reason Babs wasn't happy when Major Thomas threatened to make her late to church that Sunday morning in the 1980s was not because she was in a rush to sit in the pew and listen to Buford. She had a Sunday school class to teach. In the mid-1970s, she and several other ladies started a women's Sunday school class that endured for almost twenty years. Arnette Swift, Felicia Swinford, Patty Gumbinger, Sandi Reid, Deborah Berry, and Babs were the rotating team of teachers speaking to between 75 and 100 women every week.

The ladies of the church published a cookbook titled *Our Daily Bread* in 1979 to raise funds for Awana and its missionary, Harry Schuster. Sadly, some of the ladies who put together that cookbook and many who contributed recipes to it have passed away, but their work endures; copies of that cookbook are still in use.[83]

Today, as a continuation of that heritage, Community offers several different Sunday school classes and Bible studies for women of all ages. These meetings range from groups of young mothers meeting to support and encourage one another to a group called the Sew 'N Sews, ladies who get together weekly to create quilts and other sewn projects for members and ministries of the church.

Beau's wife, Kim, is equally as committed to prayer, but she uses modern technology to aid her in ministry. For instance, on her Facebook wall, she writes messages like this to church

---

83 Copies sold for $7. If you're ever lucky enough to get your hands on one of these cookbooks, try any recipe submitted by Shirley Menard.

members and friends: "As time goes on, I am realizing more and more the battle that is going on for our families – especially our children. I would love to pray for your kids. Just leave a note here or send me a private message. And I would love for you to pray for my kids."

Paula Brannon and her husband, Tom, first visited the church in 1972, when it was new to the Reynolds Road location. Paula says there were maybe forty or fifty people there, and she could hear their son, Paul, crying in the nursery during the entire service. She says, "I almost did not come back the following Sunday because I was afraid he would cry the whole time. I will never forget Carol Kohl and Dee Fleming, who encouraged me that first Sunday to come back and try the nursery again. We came back the following Sunday, and I didn't hear him crying. When I went to pick him up after the service, a nursery worker had walked him around the entire campus outside to keep him happy. I knew then it was where God wanted us to be. I have never forgotten the encouragement that Dee and Carol gave me and have tried to do the same for young mothers through the years."

Paula came on staff in 1998, and in January 2000, she became the church's first full-time Women's Minister. When Gary Lester retired in 2010, Paula took over his role as Pastor of Caring Ministries, and in 2011 Amy Davis came on staff as Women's Ministry Coordinator. Paula says of her job, "I am actually on my third career. I worked as an admin to various state government department heads, had my own decorating business for over twenty years, and my third and final career is here at Community. Growing up, I never dreamed God would allow me to serve Him in this way, but I am certainly glad He has brought me to this place. The last sixteen years have given my life such significance, and God has used the hurts and loss in my life to help me minister to others."

Her duties in the Caring Ministry include hospital visits, handling the Pastor-on-Call schedules, coordinating visits, and caring for members with long-term illness or death in the family. She also sees that funerals and memorial services go smoothly. "Each day is different as one crisis phone call can turn your focus from mundane administrative duties to holding the hand of a dear church member who just lost a loved one. It is a hard job, but God has blessed Community with a staff of people who don't hesitate to go when needed," she says. Whether it is matching up someone looking to give away a washer and dryer with a family in need of one or organizing the Southern tradition of providing meals for bereaved families or assisting church members in job searches, Paula and the Caring Ministry are often the hands and feet by which Community Bible Church does the day-to-day work of meeting the physical needs of the people it serves.

Throughout history, religion has been a primarily paternalistic organization, with only sporadic instances of women actually being in positions of leadership. And in many parts of the world, even today, women are treated terribly in the name of God and religion. In most American churches, men are the face of the church, while women serve in what might be termed the interior ministries, those in the background. And while church leaders often speak of helping the poor and downtrodden, it is often those behind the scenes who do the legwork involved in those caring-type ministries.

Traditionally, men have been the head of Community Bible Church, while women were the hands and the heart. But that is changing. Women now serve on the Board of Elders, and more and more, they are filling leadership positions in the congregation.

It is to Community's credit that both the exterior and interior, the being and the doing, and the out-in-front and behind-the-scenes jobs are recognized as important. And that women are valued for their contributions to the ministry.

Mom and Dad moved to Florida not long after my sister gave birth to twins named Faith and Grace. The twins were grandkids number six and seven, and two more, Joe and Kate, would be added in 2003 and 2005.

The grandchildren call my dad an interesting name. He's Fufie (pronounced Foofie) or just Fuf. It's a variation on Mom's pet name for him – Bufie -- that my daughter Morgan picked up when she was just beginning to talk.

Several years ago, I was asked to describe my dad by completing two sentences. The first sentence was, "On a good day, my dad was always . . ." The second sentence: "On a bad day, my dad was always . . ." I used the same words to complete both sentences. On a good day, my dad was always right. And on a bad day, he was (still) always right.

Fufie's never been a touchy-feely sort of guy. He's like a turtle, with a tough shell guarding a tender underbelly, only not many people ever experienced the tender underbelly. I hardly ever did, and I was his kid. He was driven, and he expected no less from those around him.

In researching for this book, I came across a document called "Certificate of Commitment." Dated February 27, 1978, and signed by Dad and by Len McWilliams, who was the Chairman of the Board of Elders at the time, the document's cover stated, "We, the pastor, staff and elders of Clayton Community Church do hereby commit ourselves to fulfill the obligations listed in Scripture and enumer-ated on the following page. We are convicted that we, the spiritual protectors of this part of Christ's body, must do all that we can to in-sure your individual spiritual growth." The inside of the document contained three possible options for each member's commitment and signature: "A Commitment of Conviction," "A Commitment of Convenience," or a "Statement of Non-Commitment." Those who signed the Commitment of Conviction promised to attend Sunday school and worship services regularly, take part in a vol-unteer ministry, set aside time each day for personal prayer and devotions, tithe their income, and consider giving an offering above the tithe as God provided. The second option, the Commitment of Convenience, meant that the person selecting it would attend wor-ship services regularly, volunteer in a church ministry, and help support the church financially. The final choice, Statement of Non-Commitment, acknowledged that the member did not commit to attending church, volunteering, or giving. It offered that mem-ber two choices: remaining a member unwilling to commit to the church or being removed from the membership rolls.

Not a single member chose to be removed from the rolls, but those who did not fill out one of the commitment forms were purged from the roll. It created an uproar in Clayton County. Some of the members who were dropped from the church roll became irate and called the local paper to complain. The paper printed an article criticizing the church for purging its member-ship roll. Ultimately, the church apologized, and the members who weren't too angry to stay away forever were reinstated.

I giggled as I read that document. It sounded just like my dad. At least, it sounded like he used to be.

These days, my parents live on the beach in St. Augustine, Florida. Fufie still goes for long "talking to God" walks, only these days the walks are on the beach. Most mornings, he stops for breakfast at a restaurant called The World Famous Oasis, a ramshackle affair like one the writer Tim Dorsey once described as looking like it is "simultaneously being constructed and torn down." Every morning, after he's read through *The Wall Street Journal*, Dad walks home with a large Styrofoam cup of coffee in his hand.[84]

The "always right" thing is gone, though, like a sand castle during high tide. I'd sensed it in the way he and my mother interacted since his retirement, but I might never have actually *seen* it if it hadn't been for my sister's little girl, Kate.

My brother, sister, and I never had the nerve to dispute him. We three children gave them nine grandchildren, and the first eight never much talked back to him.

But then came Kate. Kate is the embodiment of the nursery rhyme about the "Little girl with the little curl/right in the center of her forehead/When she was good, she was very, very good/but when she was bad, she was horrid."

The year Kate was three, the whole family managed to spend Spring Break in St. Augustine. And for the first time since my sister had four children in less than three years, the whole family went to a nice restaurant together. We had a lovely meal. The children behaved, and we ate steamed oysters while watching the sunset over the Intercoastal Waterway.

After dinner, as we made our way to the parking lot, Kate's brother, Joe, picked up a stick and started swinging it at two of his older cousins. Dad saw what was happening and moved to grab the stick from Joe, ordering in his sternest "chat-with-the-boss"

---

84 Those walks stopped for about 18 months because he was suffering from severe spinal stenosis. Thanks to successful back surgery in October 2013, he's back to his morning walks on the beach.

voice, "Joe, don't you do it!" And as we have done our whole lives, my sister, brother, and I stopped to watch him take care of the matter.

But Kate was having none of it. She saw him heading for her brother and apparently did not like the look on his face. She reached down and grabbed two handfuls of sand and threw them at him. Then this fiery little curly-headed, red-haired powerhouse yelled at the top of her lungs, "You shut up, you scoopid!"

Dad stopped. And then my mom, all ninety-five pounds and five feet of her, threw herself in between the two of them and yelled at my dad, "You're bullying a little kid. You go get in the car right now!"

And he did.

Fufie is not the same man I grew up with. Or at least, it's not how I perceived the man as I was growing up in his house. The man I grew up with was always right, and everyone, including his wife and kids, deferred to his wishes.

This man was stopped in his tracks by two angry females with a combined weight of 125 pounds. I was stunned. And so were my brother, his wife, my sister, her husband, and most of the grandchildren.

What happened? Is the Type-A personality permanently gone, replaced by a kinder, more sensitive retired man whom I struggle to recognize as my father? Or did he merely lose the tough outer shell, revealing the tender person he always was? Did moving to the beach mellow him out that much?

My Uncle Gerry says, "Buford isn't as fiery as he used to be," and it's a statement of recognition that he's a better, more enlightened version of the driven younger man he was in the church's early years. He served well, and he left knowing the place into which he'd poured his life was in capable hands. Perhaps the fire is gone simply because it's no longer needed.

One Day At a Time

Yesterday's gone, sweet Jesus,
and tomorrow may never be mine,
So for my sake, teach me to take
one day at a time.[85]

On a cold Saturday morning in February 2014, over 1,100 people packed the church auditorium for a training seminar. The event was for leaders in the Celebrate Recovery organization.

Launched in the mid-1990s at Saddleback Church in Southern California, Celebrate Recovery is a Christian program with a stated mission of helping "those struggling with hurts, habits and hang-ups by showing them the loving power of Jesus Christ through a recovery process." Today, according to the Celebrate Recovery website, the program is in over 20,000 churches around the world.

The statistics on addiction in the United States are staggering. According to The Partnership for a Drugfree America, 23.5 million Americans -- nearly one in ten -- are addicted to drugs and alcohol. And on any given day, some 700,000 people will seek treatment for an addiction.

---

[85] Written by Marijohn Wilkin and Kris Kristofferson. Published by Buckhorn Music. Used by permission.

One Day At a Time

The cover story of the November 25, 2011, issue of *Newsweek* was titled "The Sex Addiction Epidemic." The article by Chris Lee said that 40 million people (about 13% of the US population) log onto porn sites every day, and as many as nine million exhibit some form of sexually compulsive behavior and may fit the clinical definition of "sex addict." Even more telling, the number of psychologists specializing in the disorder went from 100 in 2001 to over 1,500 in 2011. The fastest growing Twelve-Step programs in the world are Sex Addicts Anonymous, Sexaholics Anonymous, and Sex and Love Addicts Anonymous.

Alcoholics Anonymous, the nation's best known recovery organization, was born out of a series of religious meetings following World War I. Bill W., the founder of AA, attended the "Oxford Group" meetings and used their messages in writing the famed Twelve-Step Program, upon which virtually every addiction and recovery program is based.

Step One says, "I recognize that my life is unmanageable and I am powerless to fix it." Step Two teaches that only a power greater than myself can fix the problem. In other words, freedom comes by admitting the problem and then looking to God for help.

In January 1999, Community Bible Church began a series of messages called "Road to Recovery" in all of its Sunday morning services. A brochure was mailed to every household in Henry County with an invitation to those services, and it included a list of the recovery groups offered at the church.

The response to that brochure and to the "Road to Recovery" messages was greater than the church's pastors and staff could have anticipated. Services were packed, and many people joined the support and recovery groups offered at the church. Most likely, the response was so great because addiction is so widespread in the American culture, and it is a devastating disease. Yet for some reason, every group that started fizzled out after a while.

During the summer of 2007, Beau looked at Jack during staff meeting and said, "Jack, how come we can't get any recovery groups going? I have a lot of people coming to me with serious needs, and I really don't know what to do with them."

"I'm not sure why he was talking to me because I didn't know anything about recovery groups," Jack says, but when Beau suggested that he check out Celebrate Recovery, Jack's answer was, "That's a good idea, and I can definitely do that."

He began by visiting Celebrate Recovery meetings at East Ridge Community Church in Covington, Georgia, which was where the Southeastern director of Celebrate Recovery went to church. "Every Thursday night, I tried to take a group with me to see and experience the meetings," he says. Not long after Jack started visiting those meetings, his wife, Diana, ran into Toney Jones at a grocery store near their home in McDonough. Toney was the Youth Ranch kid who had taken over the director's job from Buford in the early 1970s. Although he'd occasionally visited the church and had been instrumental in the building of the Jeremiah Justice Youth Building in 1997, he had been away from the church and the Lord for thirty years.

Between 1983 and 2006, Toney owned and operated six very successful bars in the Atlanta area. Although he had everything he could ever want, he knew something was missing. One of the bars, O'Haras on Tara Boulevard in Jonesboro, began adopting families to provide for at Christmas, and Toney realized one day as they were delivering gifts that it was the happiest he'd been in ages.

He began to think that he needed a new life's work. He was pretty sure, though, given his past, that if it involved the church, he was "only worthy to hold doors open and greet people." And he was scared of selling the bars for two reasons: he wouldn't have any friends and he wouldn't be able to make a living.

He went on vacation to Nicaragua in order to sit on the beach and figure things out. While there, he saw little children scrounging for food in the dump that served the capitol city of Managua. He decided that he wanted his life to count for more than just being a good bartender. He came home and put all of his bars up for sale.

That day in the grocery store, Toney was buying plastic champagne glasses for the final party at his last bar, Memories, located on Hudson Bridge Road, just one exit north of the church on I-75. In a few hours, he would be completely out of the bar business, and he began confiding in Diana that he had decided he wanted to do something meaningful with the rest of his life. Diana told him Jack was starting a new ministry at the church called Celebrate Recovery and that she was certain Jack would love to have Toney's help.

Toney responded, "Well, this was probably a providential meeting because I know Jack don't know nothing about alcohol and drugs. I might need to help out." The very next night, Toney went with Jack to a Celebrate Recovery meeting, and he became instrumental in helping the program at Community get off the ground.

Over the next six or seven months, Jack says, as he took different people to see the meetings in Covington, they developed a leadership team. "We did a lot of preparations, a lot of training, and the week after Easter 2008, we launched Celebrate Recovery on a Thursday night to a packed chapel," Jack says.

The Thursday night meetings have four separate segments. The first hour is a fellowship meal. Then, from 7 to 8 p.m. is the main meeting, which consists of worship and either a fifteen-minute testimony or a teaching on the Twelve Steps. The third hour is for open share groups, which are issue-specific and gender-specific. For example, there are groups for chemical dependency for men, chemical dependency for women, co-dependency for men, and co-dependency for women, plus sexual addiction groups, depression groups, and a few others. There is also a newcomers group, which consists of a 45-minute meeting to give visitors information about Celebrate Recovery. Finally, once the group meetings are finished, everyone gathers in the atrium for coffee, desserts, and fellowship. Approximately sixteen different groups currently meet on Thursday nights.

In addition to the Thursday night meeting, Jack says, the church hosts Twelve-Step groups meeting on other nights of the week, typically Wednesday or Sunday. Those groups are also gender-specific. Members work through four small booklets, and it takes about nine months to complete a Step study.

"We've seen tremendous life changes through Twelve-Step groups," Jack says, adding that it's a tremendous process for people to go through in healing their hurts, habits, and hang-ups. "We've seen great success and progress in people's lives. We found also that Celebrate Recovery is a leadership factory, and what pastor doesn't want to hear about more volunteers and more leaders? So we're going strong. We'll celebrate our seventh anniversary in April 2015, and we have about seventy volunteers every Thursday night who help lead Twelve-Step groups."

Toney Jones remarried in 2008. He and his wife, Debbie, now spend half of every year in Nicaragua, where they host mission teams who travel from churches around the United States to help him feed children in Nicaragua.

One Day At a Time

❊ ❊ ❊

Comedian Bob Newhart has a classic skit in which he plays a therapist. A woman comes to see him, and after explaining that he charges $5 for the first five minutes and then nothing after that, the woman is thrilled. She starts her session by telling the therapist that she is afraid of being buried alive in a box. Her fear is so bad, she says, that she is unable to get on elevators, go through tunnels, or even enter a house – "anything boxy."

"So what you're saying is you're claustrophobic."

"Yes, that's it," the woman admits.

"Well, Katherine, I'm going to say two words to you that I want you to take home and incorporate into your life," Newhart says, and then he waits for her to pull out a notepad and a pen. When she's ready, he leans forward in his chair and shouts, "STOP IT!"

The woman acts confused and asks him to explain himself. "STOP IT. Just STOP IT!" he repeats.

She then tells the doctor she's bulimic. "I stick my hand down my throat and make myself throw up."

"STOP IT!"

"I have self-destructive relationships with men."

"STOP IT! You want to be with a man, don't you?

"Yes."

"Well, then, STOP IT!"

It's a funny skit that begs the question of whether or not it's possible to just "STOP IT" when it comes to addiction. Some people make multiple trips through rehab -- a price tag upwards of $1,000 a day is not uncommon -- only to come out and go right back to the behavior that is hell bent on killing them. The relapse rate is as high as 90% for some addictions. For alcoholism, the statistics are grim: if maintaining sobriety for five years is the standard, then less than four percent of recovering alcoholics are successful.[86]

So is it even possible to simply "STOP IT"?

About a year ago, I was having lunch with my grandfather, Horace Adams, who was ninety at the time. We were talking about the prevalence of addiction in our society, and he told me a story I'd never heard before.

I've already mentioned that my grandmother was one of eleven children – six girls and five boys – who grew up in a valley north of Rome, Georgia, during the Depression. Their father was a poor sharecropper, and their mother died in childbirth when Grandmom was three, leaving her older siblings to help raise her and the baby, Douglas, until their father remarried.

Two of her brothers came home from World War Two and spent the rest of their lives as alcoholics, and her father begin drinking heavily at the end of his life to ease the pain of his terminal cancer. Naturally, she was afraid of alcohol, and so it's no huge surprise that when Granddad came home from the war, she promised to leave him if he ever drank. He never did, but he says they gave away cigarettes to the G.I.s during the war, and when he came home, he was, as he puts it, "hooked" on cigarettes.

It was a quarter of a century later, in the early 1970s, the best he can remember, that he was driving down Reynolds Road one day and thinking about how much money he spent every month on cigarettes and tobacco for his pipe. "I decided it was expensive, and it really was nasty, so I stopped my truck on the side of the road, and I got all my cigarettes and my pipe and my tobacco off the dash of my truck, and I threw it in the woods there on Reynolds' property."

"Did you ever smoke again?"

---

86 According to the website addictioninfo.org.

He laughed. "Nah. I don't understand these people who say they can't quit. I just decided I didn't want to smoke any more, and I didn't."

So there you have it, someone who just stopped. It's possible. But for those who need help from others, I think that Celebrate Recovery is one of the best things going. For starters, it's free. The people who show up to the meetings on Thursday nights want to be there, which is a significant marker of success in achieving and maintaining sobriety. The organization has developed its own version of the Twelve Steps, which are modeled after the traditional AA Steps with Scripture validating and supporting each step. Like their slogan says, Celebrate Recovery is a safe place to heal.

Higher Ground

My heart has no desire to stay
Where doubts arise and fears dismay;
Tho' some may dwell where these abound,
My prayer, my aim, is higher ground[87]

The Religious Freedom Restoration Act (RFRA) was passed in 1993 as a means of preventing laws that might burden a person's right to the free exercise of religion. That law was overturned in 1997. It was replaced by the Religious Land Use and Institutionalized Persons Act (RLUIPA), which was passed in both branches of Congress by a unanimous consent in voice votes[88] and signed into law by President Bill Clinton in September 2000.

RLUIPA is a strange law that prohibits burdens being placed on prisoners that might keep them from worshipping as they please while giving churches a way around restrictive zoning laws. Essentially, the law provides churches and religious organizations with the same authority over their property that an individual citizen would have.

For the first half of its existence, the ministry had a good working relationship with local government, mostly because local officials liked the positive influence of the organization in the

---

87 Lyrics by Johnson Oatman, Jr.
88 No objection was raised, so no recorded vote was necessary.

community. But the move to Henry County meant a slight shift in its rock-solid standing with local officials. In February 1993, the church applied to the Henry County Planning Committee for a permit to place two modular units on church property in order to provide space for four classrooms. Although there was no opposition present at the meeting, the request was denied. The church appealed the decision, and a hearing before the Henry County Board of Commissioners was set for March 16, 1993. The church asked its members to write letters to their commissioners urging them to reconsider that decision. Those units were ultimately approved.

Eighteen months later, in the fall of 1994, the church received a permit to put two more portables on the property in anticipation of opening a school campus in Henry County. Two months later, the county inspector approved the classrooms but informed the church that they had ninety days to apply costly skirting to the units. The church appealed that requirement on the basis that Henry County schools with portable units were not required to have skirting around them, but that appeal went unrecognized for over a year. In January 1996, the Planning and Zoning board denied the appeal on the basis that they had no authority over the public schools. The church then appealed to the Henry County Board of Commissioners, and the issue was set to be addressed at their February 6, 1996, meeting. The church again asked its members to contact their commissioners and urge them not to hold the church to different standards than it held county schools. Ultimately, the county commission approved the modular units with no skirting, but both incidences were a sign to the church that the political climate as it pertained to religious organizations was changing just a bit.

In the mid-2000s, rather than renting out Tara Stadium and hiring a famous Gospel singer, the church began celebrating the

Fourth of July with a huge event on its own property. Called Freedom Fest, the celebration featured patriotic music, fireworks, and, perhaps in a minor nod to July 4, 1776, chicken dinners.

Freedom Fest attracted thousands of people, most of whom loved the celebration. But a woman who lived near the church was not happy about the crowds and the noise. During the 2007 celebration, she called 911 to complain. The police responded after the first call but left when they realized the church had the proper permits for the event. The woman proceeded to call 911 over and over. Finally, after about the tenth call to 911, police went to the woman's house and told her one more call would put her in big trouble. Still, it created a new enemy for the church.

The church subsequently purchased two homes on six acres across Mt. Olive Road with the intention of tearing down the houses and using the land to build ball fields for the school. In early 2009, the church hired a member named Danny Agee, who owned a grading company called McDonough Development, to clear the land for those fields. Agee filled out the zoning application, and he went with the school's headmaster, Fred Banke, to the Henry County Commission's zoning hearing.

The Commissioners were nervous about approving that zoning because any zoning changes in the county usually came under fire. That night, it sounded as if they were going to deny the request until they began discussing RLUIPA and decided that the church had the right to use that property for ball fields.

But they demanded some concessions from the church and school in order to make the zoning change more palatable to the neighborhood. The church had to construct a fence around the property, and there could be no lights at the fields. Of course, the standard construction regulations (i.e. silt fences) still applied to the process.

The price of pulpwood was high at that time, so the church sold the wood on the property to a pulpwood company. Like pulpwooders do, they left the stumps. After the job was completed, a county agent named Rex Dickey came by to inspect it, and he suggested that the church grind up the stumps and spread the mulch across the site in order to keep it from being too muddy. The church complied with his suggestion.

A woman whose property backed up to the site became enraged when the grading process started, and she began calling the newspapers to accuse the Henry County Commission of being paid off by the church. When that came to nothing, she called the Georgia Environmental Protection Division and complained. A woman from the EPD visited the site during a torrential downpour and videotaped mud puddles forming in the rain.

Beau soon received a summons to appear in front of the EPD's Mountain District.[89] An official from Henry County – Rex Dickey's boss – went with him. "We showed up at their office near the Atlanta airport," Beau says, "and sat down with a man named Bert Langley. The man said we'd violated several environmental laws, and then he told us we were looking at a six-figure fine."

With the Henry County official backing him, Beau said to the man, "But we followed the county's guidelines, and they have approved everything we've done."

Langeley's response was, "Tough. It's your property and your fine."

The church's insurance company quickly hired lawyers, who of course argued that the church was protected by RLUIPA. In addition, they argued that since the EPD hires local governments

---

89 The Mountain District of Georgia's EPD covers Cartersville and the Atlanta area. Langley is the coordinator for the EPD district offices.

to enforce its rules, the EPD couldn't fine the church for following the guidelines of a county government that they were employing.

The two sides battled for two full years, and in 2011, they went to arbitration. The church was ordered to pay a fine of $10,000.

But the battle wasn't over yet. Their argument fueled by the fact the church paid a fine, the owners of six properties neighboring the church hired an environmental attorney and filed a civil suit claiming that the church had destroyed the nature in the woods behind the six acres.

One woman claimed in a deposition that a black panther that had lived on her property for years disappeared after the property was graded. Another man, who was facing foreclosure and whose property didn't even adjoin the church's six acres, claimed that mud had seeped into his pond, thereby prohibiting him from enjoying his own property.

Both sides went before a county arbitrator, but they were unable to settle. They were ordered by a district court judge to appear before a federal arbitrator at the Richard B. Russell Federal building in downtown Atlanta. The suit was settled for an undisclosed amount in the fall of 2012, three years after Henry County approved zoning for the project.

While the amount of money each family received is undisclosed, the settlement ultimately allowed the church to build the ball fields (with lights!), and the families involved in the civil suit have agreed never to sue the church again.

There was a time when people held churches in high esteem. The church was "God's House." People didn't mess with God, and that meant they wouldn't dream of suing a church.

Higher Ground

The woman who initially accused the Zoning Board of being in cahoots with the church and then called the Environmental Protection Division was the same person who solicited her neighbors to join with her in a lawsuit against the church. One neighbor who was contacted was horrified by the suggestion and said, "Oh, no, I would never sue a church."

I'm not saying churches are infallible. There have been horrors perpetrated and covered up by the church in the name of God throughout the ages, and those evils should not go unpunished. But suing a church because you don't want a baseball field backing up to your property? Who does that? Did these people not see *Field of Dreams*?

And do they not know what could have been built behind them? Ten years ago, residents of the Oak Grove subdivision in McDonough, just a few miles away from the church, fought a landfill expansion behind their neighborhood. The landfill, which was owned by a former county commissioner, had been there before any zoning ordinances were in place, and the question was whether or not the expansion fell under the current zoning laws. I don't know about you, but I'd much rather see baseball diamonds than dump trucks from my back porch.

I suggested the church turn the property into an organic pig farm. Ten to fifteen sows fit comfortably on an acre, so the church could host a nice hog killing/covered-dish dinner every January and then feed the multitudes at Freedom Fest some delicious free barbeque.

The real test of the "I AM LOVED at Community Bible Church" catchphrase, I suppose, is whether or not we can extend that sentiment to those who we feel have wronged us. Obviously, I'm not where I should be, although I could find it in my heart to walk a plate of free barbeque over to those neighbors.

One Day

Living, He loved me; dying, He saved me;
Buried, He carried my sins far away;
Rising, He justified freely forever
One day He's coming, O glorious day![90]

The weather forecast for Easter weekend 2014 predicted thunderstorms across the southeastern United States. To a preacher planning for the biggest crowds of the year, the radar couldn't have looked much worse. Sure enough, a line of thunderstorms rolled across Georgia and Florida beginning on Good Friday morning, bringing with it tornado watches and a great deal of rain. The front settled in and threatened to ruin Community Bible Church's Easter Eggstravaganza, which was planned for the afternoon before Easter.

Hundreds of volunteers had been working for weeks stuffing candy into 52,000 plastic eggs. Rain was still falling an hour before the hunt was to begin. When asked if this was going to be his "July 4," Beau laughed and said, "If only fifty kids show up, those kids are going to get a lot of candy!" By 5:00, the rain had stopped, but enough of a drizzle was falling to warrant umbrellas. The eggs were "hidden" across the church parking lots because the ball fields were soggy. Despite the dismal weather,

---

90 Words by J. Wilbur Chapman

hundreds of children and their parents showed up to claim their Easter candy.

The next morning, nearly one hundred people gathered for a sunrise service in St. Augustine Beach, Florida. Wind and a heavy drizzle had forced the crowd to gather in a neighborhood pool pavilion, and a thick cloud cover meant there was no hope of seeing the sun rising over the edge of the Atlantic Ocean. Because of the change in location, the service started ten minutes late. It began with the crowd singing "Amazing Grace" *a cappella*. Dressed in a silk Tommy Bahama shirt and khaki shorts, Buford Adams greeted the crowd and then opened with a couple of jokes, including one of his favorite lines: "As Elizabeth Taylor said to each of her seven husbands, I won't keep you long." He read the Easter story from John 20 and then pulled his wallet from his back pocket as a prop for the same illustration he's been using for nearly fifty years, the "Hand Gesture." *Let this hand represent you and me, and this hand represent God. Let my wallet represent sin . . .*

Three hours later and three hundred and fifty miles away, his son, Beau, greeted a packed crowd in one of Community's multiple Easter morning services. "Turn to a couple of people around you and say, 'Welcome to the Happy Jesus church!'"[91]

Beau's message lasted a little longer than his father's, but he used a version of his dad's old sermon preparation formula. With the words to a traditional Easter song, "One Day," as his outline, he used five points and a poem to explain the message of Easter.

As he began winding down, he told the story of Jimmy Nidifer, the boy on his high school soccer team who, along with

---

91 One year earlier, a church member had invited a friend to celebrate Easter at Community. "Oh, you go to that happy Jesus church, huh?" the friend had said, intending it as an insult.

his cousin, was killed so many years ago in a car accident. Weeks before, Beau had received a message from a church member asking if Beau would be willing to talk to the younger brother of the cousin who died in the accident with Jimmy. Jason Nidifer came to see Beau and told him about the destructive path his life had taken in the years since that tragic accident.

"Jason trusted Christ as his Savior at Celebrate Recovery," Beau announced to that Easter Sunday crowd, who erupted in applause.

My son, Hunter, was a senior in high school when we held the first St. Augustine Beach Easter sunrise service, in 2013. Dad used the Liz Taylor line that morning, also. Hunter giggled softly and said, "Fufie loves that joke, doesn't he?" I realized in that moment that my son thought Dad used that line every time he spoke because he had heard my dad speak only once before, at a camp for teenagers.

My daughters had been old enough to sit in the church services and hear my dad speak before he retired, but by the time Hunter had outgrown the nursery, Beau was the senior pastor.

Months later, at a Youth Ranch reunion, Jack Bartlett introduced me to Frank and Martha Houston, former Forest Park High School teachers who also volunteered during the early days of the Youth Ranch. Frank told me he'd taken pity on Dad and his lousy guitar playing and had helped for several years with the music. He looked at me and said, "Your dad and I had this thing. He told the same joke every week, and at one point in the joke, he would fling his right arm. The first few times, it caught me in the face. After that, I learned to duck, and we had this perfect synchronization."

When I told Dad that at least two people – Hunter and Frank Houston – were onto him and his penchant for repeating jokes, he laughed and said, "You gotta recycle a good clean joke. They're hard to come by."

I arrived ten minutes early for the 2014 Easter sunrise service, and I stood in the back as 6:30 came and went, watching in amusement to see how my dad would handle the delayed start time. In over forty years of Sundays, I'd never seen my dad start a service late, and I could see him fidgeting as people were still streaming in at 6:37. At 6:40, he made his way to the front and, pointing to an empty chair right in front of him, said, "There's a five dollar seat here for anyone who wants it." Because I was standing up in the back, I felt all eyes on me, so in a moment of complete *déjà vu*, I found myself seated on the front row and looking up at my dad as he once again delivered a Sunday sermon.

When it was over, I went home and pulled up Community-BibleChurch.com on my computer. I watched as my brother told one of the same jokes my dad had just told. I listened to him say essentially the same thing our father had just said, and I had to smile at the irony of my dad's service that morning being more casual than Beau's. Then my brother did something my dad had avoided his entire career -- Beau baptized someone during the service.

When he finished telling the story of Jimmy Nidifer and his younger cousin, Jason, Beau walked off the stage and stood next to a portable baptistry that had been placed in front of the stage just for the occasion. I sat up in my seat, wondering how my brother was planning to baptize someone right in the middle of his message. He wasn't wearing fishing waders! His lavalier microphone was still clipped to his shirt! Jason climbed over the edge and stood in the pool, while Beau, still standing outside the pool, took Jason's hands in his and said the words I've heard a thousand times: "I baptize you now, my brother, in the name of the Father, the Son, and the Holy Spirit. Buried in the likeness of His death, and raised in the likeness of His resurrection to walk in newness of life." For thirty years, my dad baptized by lowering people backwards into the water and then muscling them back up, the way I'm sure he'd seen it done his whole life. But as Beau spoke those words, Jason bent his knees to immerse himself in the water, then straightened his legs and stood back up.

It was a perfect metaphor for the church's role in our lives. Sometimes we need someone to pull us out of the depths. Other times, like He did with Noah, God gives us a vision and the means to build a vessel by which we save ourselves. Ultimately, the church's role is to work itself out of a job by showing its members how to have a vision and the means to build our own boats. At Community, no matter who you are or where you've been, you will find someone willing to love you enough to pull you out of the mire. And if you stick around long enough, you'll learn to develop a deep and personal relationship with God so that you can also help yourself.

I struggled with the title of this book for the whole time I was writing it. I played with "Three Points and a Poem," "Amazing Grace," and a hundred variations on the theme of community. But I kept coming back to the idea that this book is really about discovering what made people keep coming back week after week. One morning as I was walking the beach and mulling over possible titles, I remembered those blue bumper stickers from long ago: "I AM LOVED at Clayton Community Church." Because isn't that the one thing we have to comprehend, that we are absolutely loved by God? And where else on this earth are people going to get that message if it's not in His church?

I called my brother to tell him that I'd finally found the title. "It's 'I AM LOVED at Community Bible Church,'" I said.

He chuckled and said, "That's really it. That's why people keep coming back." And then said, "Do you remember Jason, the guy I baptized on Easter Sunday? Do you know why he came to see me and came to Celebrate Recovery? His family knew way back then that we cared about them. And he came back to Community because he knew that he would be loved here."

Amazing Grace

When we've been there ten thousand years,
Bright shining as the sun,
We've no less days to sing God's praise
Than when we'd first begun[92]

The Great Recession of 2008 officially lasted from December 2007 until June 2009. During that time, America lost 8.4 million jobs, roughly 6.1 percent of all paid employment. It was the worst loss of jobs since the Great Depression. The result, of course, was a drop in family incomes and an increase in poverty. For the church it meant a huge downturn in contributions while requests for financial assistance increased.

This was not the first recession that had affected the church. In fact, every recession during the church's history had meant cuts in spending. But this one was much deeper, and Beau faced the difficult decision of how to cut the church's budget. The options were to cut programs or to cut payroll expenses. Thankfully, under the wise leadership of the finance committee and the Board of

---

92 "Amazing Grace" was written by John Newton, an English slave ship captain who left the slave trade and later became a minister. He used the song's original lyrics to illustrate a sermon in January 1773. The lyrics printed here, which make up the song's fifth stanza, were added to a version of "Amazing Grace" in Harriet Beecher Stowe's novel *Uncle Tom's Cabin* (1852) and have been attributed to songwriter John P. Rees.

Elders, the church survived and has even thrived. But as all difficult situations do, this economic downturn brought about great change at Community Bible Church.

For starters, the church is now more focused on the helping ministries. The Urban Hug Team regularly takes pans of homemade spaghetti to different locations around Atlanta and serves food to the homeless. Maximum Impact Love is a ministry that shares the love of Christ with people on Fulton Industrial Boulevard. The church supports halfway houses for both men and women recovering from addiction. Small groups formed during the 40 Days of Community Campaigns, celebrated during the weeks leading up to Easter Sunday, focus on service projects in the community like painting a children's shelter, throwing a baby shower for an expectant mother in need, or volunteering with Habitat for Humanity.

Another change at Community has occurred in the way the church has grown. Jack Bartlett points out that during the years Buford was the senior pastor, the church averaged one new building every three years. "Year one was the fundraising, year two was the design phase, and year three was the actual construction," he says, adding, "If you look at Buford's personality profile, he's what's known as a 'developer.'[93] That's what he did here at the church." When it comes to the Henry County move, he says, "Even though it wasn't popular with a lot of people at the time, looking back, I think we all see that Buford was a genius when it came to seeing the direction the church needed to go and taking us in that direction."

---

93 According to the Performax Personality Profile System, developers are "strong individualists who continually seek new horizons. . . . Developers are able to bypass convention and often come up with imaginative and innovative solutions. . . they have high expectations of others and can be critical when their standards are not met."

Although Beau's manner of growing the church is a bit different, it still is based upon the church's longtime purpose statement: "To develop a dynamic church through the grace and power of Christ dedicated to the worship of God, to equipping the body for daily ministry, and to evangelizing the lost, both locally and beyond." And their styles of ministry diverge in other ways: in joking that he was always waiting for the right pastor to show up at Community, Buford was saying that his tenure in the ministry was a calling. By comparison, Beau considers the church his passion. And while his dad's personality could be described as more goal-oriented, Beau's is more focused on people.

One Sunday morning in February 2014, a little four-year-old girl named Sofi ran up to Beau after the morning services and grabbed his legs. "Hey, Pastor Beau, I saw you on stage!"

"You did? Why didn't you come see me?"

"I have a boyfriend!" Sofi responded.

"You do? Who?"

"Guess who?"

"Zacharia?"

"No."

Beau rattled off several other random boy names, and to each Sofi shook her head no. Finally, she said, "It's Justin Bieber!"

"Justin Bieber? Really? I know who that is," Beau said.

"Well, can you dance like Justin Bieber?" Beau broke out in a few Justin Bieber moves, and she said, "Well can you sing like Justin Bieber?"

At that, to Sofi's great amusement, Beau began belting out "Baby, baby, baby . . . ."[94]

---

94 I hope it goes without saying that the world would be a much better place with more Beaus and fewer Biebers.

Beau is an unfailing optimist who consistently looks for the good in people, and that story is reminiscent of the one in Matthew 19 when people tried to keep some children from bothering Jesus. He would have none of it because, as He said, "Little kids are heaven."[95]

The word "beyond," the last one of the church's long-standing purpose statement, has taken on a slightly different meaning at the church these days. While Community has shifted away from sending missionaries to live in other parts of the world, the church began streaming the Sunday morning services online in 2009. On Sundays, it reaches a new crowd via the Internet. Viewers hail from every state and from several foreign countries. In addition, through John Maxwell's Equip Ministry, Beau travels twice a year to a foreign country – Brazil, England, Portugal, and India to date -- to train pastors, so the message is still being spread, just in a different way. In a sense, he's come full circle, returning regularly to the country where he received his pastoral training and passing it on to a new generation of pastors.

Community is also intentionally mutigenerational and multicultural. In an article about current church growth strategies, church growth researcher and strategist Ed Stetzer, Ph.D., mentions Community. He writes:

> The church offers multiple types of worship services designed to reach certain target groups of people, says Lead Pastor Beau Adams. "But we feel it is essential that everyone fellowship with people from all backgrounds and all generations." Beyond the church service, Community Bible Church

---

[95] I'm paraphrasing, of course, but I'm pretty sure that's what Jesus meant when he said of children "for of such is the kingdom of Heaven." (Matthew 19:14, KJV)

fosters multigenerational relationships in other ways with intergenerational outreaches and activities.

The church fills a void prominent throughout Western culture where the families often live a significant distance from grandparents. By connecting senior adults with the children of Community Bible, attendees are forming non-blood-related families as the young and old join together in activities like fishing. While many churches today focus their efforts and resources on drawing and keeping young families, churches like . . . Community Bible have discovered that engaging and connecting all generations leads to both attendance and spiritual growth.

Perhaps one of its grandest accomplishments is this: the church that was arguably started as a reaction to an African-American man being denied membership in an all-white Atlanta church is now considered the most welcoming church in Atlanta for mixed-race families. Mario Arnold, an Elder in the church, is African-American, and his wife, Deborah, is white. Mario says mixed-race couples feel at home in the church because "no one is looking at us funny."

From 2007-09, Community Bible Church was on *Outreach* magazine's annual list of "100 Fastest Growing Churches in America." To make the list, a church had to have an average Sunday morning attendance of at least one thousand. According to Stetzer, who is part of the LifeWay research group producing the *Outreach* lists, by 2013, the churches making the list averaged at least seven thousand members. He says, "That doesn't mean more churches are meeting in larger groups at one time in one place; the opposite may be true. While churches are getting larger, attendees are often not unified in one location as more mega churches add satellite sites."

Beau agrees. "The recession of 2008 showed us that we're more stable as we decentralize. We have to get away from being just one property, one big box with everyone there." The church consistently bumps Buford's eighty percent capacity rule. With services in both the chapel and auditorium at 9:30 and 11:00, there's no room to add an additional service. Yet there won't be new building programs at 2001 Jodeco Road every few years. Rather than constructing a new worship center, the church now focuses on branching out into local communities and beginning daughter churches in new locations. New congregations are currently meeting in Peachtree City, a suburb southwest of Atlanta and -- to punctuate the idea of having come full circle – in Morrow, only a couple of miles from the old Reynolds Road campus.

Beau says of the church's strategy for growth, "The primary avenues we use to bring people IN are weekend services and community outreach events. The Assimilation Team distributes letters to all first- and second-time visitors and places personal phone calls to every first-timer within a 24-to-48-hour period. Once a person comes IN, we encourage them to grow UP in their faith through small groups, caring ministries and our membership class. Once people come IN and begin growing UP, we send them OUT to impact others and contribute to the cycle of bringing new people back IN. Our OUT Team focuses on missions, service and community sports programs. Ultimately we rely on God to move in the hearts of our people as they are introduced to Christ and grow closer to Him."

Buford explains the church's history this way: "It has been said that there are three things that will destroy a church – changing location, changing worship style, and changing a long-term founding pastor for someone new. Community Bible Church experienced all of those changes between 1992 and 2002, and we survived. In fact, the church is much larger and more dynamic than it has ever been. The Lord absolutely knows what He is doing, and I feel grateful that we had the foresight to understand the change that was coming and to get ahead of it."

His son, a new leader for a new generation, summarizes the history of the church with these words: "The only thing that doesn't change at Community is the fact that we're always changing. Change *is* our culture."

After starting this book with a story about the Georgia Environmental Protection Division, I was tempted to end with another one – the ball fields -- and say something about having come full circle. It seemed a better ending than one filled with numbers and statistics on the church's growth, for stopping with stats seemed, in essence, to be saying, *the numbers prove that the church is successful, end of story.* But I think I know how to put those numbers in perspective.

My grandmother, Glennis Adams, died in June 2001, eleven days after being diagnosed with pancreatic cancer. Since she was one of the church's first members, and because she and my granddad were the first ever to financially support the ministry here at Community Bible Church, I want to end this fifty-year history with her words.

One of her favorite sayings was, "One hundred years from now, is anyone going to care?" For example, when I commented that it was hard to keep a house clean with toddlers, she told me it was more important to spend that time playing with my kids, adding, "One hundred years from now, is anyone going to care if your house was clean?"

As a matter of fact, when asked for her opinion about most anything, she often responded, "Is anyone going to care a hundred years from now?"

When it comes to numbers, I honestly don't think anyone will care how many people were in the pews on any given Sunday or how much the offering was. For example, it wasn't the hundreds of car count number sheets in old files that interested me as I conducted research for this book. I needed stories, not numbers. Stories about people are what make for interesting reading because people matter more than things and statistics.

I doubt I'll be around in 2065 to ask the question if anyone still cares that in 1965 a young couple sat on Coke crates next to a cracked swimming pool singing and sharing the Gospel with teenagers, but this I do know: fifty years after this ministry started, thousands of people care that Horace Adams wrote his son a letter asking if he wanted to move home and start a youth ministry. We care that a $1,000 donation by retired judge started a Christian school that has educated students from all over the world. Some of us still cheer a little teenager girl taking a hilariously courageous stand against fundamentalism. It still matters that a new youth minister with experience as an EMT saved a teenager's life. We care that this church gives twelve percent of its annual income to missions. And we care that a church congregation was brave enough to change its location in order to reach one of the fastest-growing communities in the country.

I found a letter in my parents' files written to my mom's twin sister, Sandy, in 1966, just after Joe McCracken had threatened to foreclose on the Youth Ranch property. My aunt had expressed concern, and this was my dad's reply: "We're not discouraged. It's just that we are going to have to get about $850 worth of back rent and taxes paid or close up. I don't think it is a good testimony to be behind like this. If the Lord supplies to whatever is honoring and pleasing to Him, then the reverse must also be true, that if He doesn't supply then it is evident that what you are doing is not pleasing to Him. So there are two main courses to take: 1. Operate as usual without the Lord's blessing using schemes to raise money or 2. Change your operation either by letting the Lord supply or just forget the whole business."

In other words, Mom and Dad had come to the point of surrender, and we now know that God made a way for the ministry to continue and to thrive. And that, I believe, is the real story of Community Bible Church. From figuring out a cost-effective way to clear a ceiling of asbestos to hacking out a path through the woods so that teenagers could put on a Halloween Trail and earn their way to camp, this place has always been about allowing God to make a way, even if that way seemed ridiculous at the time. In fact, the more "unchurchlike" an idea seemed, the better it usually worked! Although it's become somewhat of a cliché, letting go and letting God is a good way of explaining the church's history.

This ministry began with a handwritten letter from Horace Adams to his son. Horace is 91, and he still drives himself to church most Sunday mornings. He remains faithful in his giving. He prefers to hear Beau or Jack preach because he says that with his questionable hearing, they're the only two whom he can completely understand. Even so, he usually makes his way to the smaller chapel service because he doesn't "much care for that 'new' music"; the old hymns are the ones with meaning for him. He's been known to stand up and walk out if one of the younger pastors in the chapel gets a bit long-winded and goes past noon. He is, after all, an Adams, and we have a strong conviction that beating the Presbyterians to the Piccadilly Cafeteria (or in Granddad's case, Kentucky Fried Chicken) is God's will on a Sunday afternoon.

I see my granddad as a metaphor for what Community Bible Church should be – strong, decent, good to its very core, solid, committed, generous, and single-minded in its dedication to God and those who are part of the church family. He established a legacy that his son and grandson are certainly perpetuating, and we all would do well to follow that lead. In his final days, he's doing what I hope to do: he's finishing well.

Community Bible Church has seen the hand of God at work for fifty years. Fifty miraculous years. May there be many more.

Ten (plus a bonus) Principles of Success Based on the History of Community

Ask – In Matthew 7:7, Jesus says, "Ask, and it will be given to you" (NIV). The "it" of that verse doesn't really matter. The point is that when we acknowledge we need help, the asking is what opens us to receiving. Remember Buford calling the Chairman of the Clayton County Commissioners, Charlie Griswell, and asking him if he would send over earth-moving equipment to help the Youth Ranch? That story is a powerful metaphor for what happens when we simply ask for what we need – God moves Heaven and earth to help us. To this day, new members to Community are asked for their help in filling volunteer positions around the church. And every week, those needs are met simply because people are, for the most part, generous and kind-hearted. People naturally want to help others, and sometimes all it takes is for someone to ask for their help. So asking is the best way to ensure that you'll receive.

Bend – In other words, be flexible. If you plan for months to celebrate the nation's Bicentennial by bringing in a famous Gospel singer and giving away 10,000 chicken dinners, and your plans are literally washed away, then find someone else who can use those dinners and laugh because you're going to get a lot of mileage out of the story in the next thirty or forty years.

Some of the most dangerous words ever spoken in a church (or even in our own lives) are these: "This is the way we've always done it." Thankfully, when the inspector from the EPA uttered similar words to Dr. Sturcken during the asbestos removal, his response – "Are we doing it wrong?" – was perfect. Most often, there's more than one good way to do anything, but you'll never learn differently if you rigidly stick to what you already know.

Be Creative – Arguably, the Atlanta Youth Ranch would never have survived its first two years if Buford hadn't been able to talk the football coaches at Hapeville High School into having summer practices at camp in Boca Raton. In other words, Buford's creative response – "Bring the whole team and all your coaches" – likely set the course for the Youth Ranch and the church. He came up with a creative solution, and only afterwards did he worry about how he was going to afford it. Creativity often means dreaming big while refusing to allow the censorship of practicality into the equation. Most often, those grand dreams find a way to become a reality if we nourish them by simply believing God's promise that "with man this is impossible, but with God all things are possible" (Matthew 19:26, NLT).

Detach – Job 1:21 eloquently describes the attitude of detachment: "The Lord gave and the Lord has taken away. Blessed be the name of the Lord" (NASB). When Len McWilliams told Buford he had taken control of the school and was not going to move to Henry County, Buford responded by shrugging his shoulders and walking away. These days, Community Christian School is bigger than ever, and not many people even know the story of how the school and church parted ways nearly twenty years ago. It could have become a huge battle, and many people would have been hurt in the process.

The illustration is a common one these days, but it seems to have first appeared as a folk legend known as *The Boy and the Filberts*. Another version, this time using a monkey, is included in Indries Shah's 1967 *Tales of the Dervishes*. Monkey or boy, it doesn't matter; the point of the story is that an easy way to make a trap is to put something valuable in the bottom of a jar. By grabbing it, a boy or a monkey forms a fist bigger than the jar's mouth. The moral, of course, is that holding on too tightly to things is a trap. Detachment is simply an easier way to live our lives.

Expect Good Things – Get this: God didn't put us here to suffer. We're here to enjoy our lives. Jesus told us as much in John 10:10: "I have come that they may have life, and that they may have it more abundantly" (NKJV).

Pick up any primer on quantum physics these days, and this is the gist of the book: the particles that make up an atom only exist as the potential to become particles until a scientist looks for them. Paying attention to them is what brings them into existence. By extension, what we pay attention to – what we expect – is what we get. The Psalmist explained it this way: "For as [a man] thinks in his heart, so *is* he" (NKJV). Why not live your life thinking about all the things that can go right rather than what can go wrong? Why not simply expect good things to happen? Doesn't that feel better?

When Beau walked into Chick-Fil-A headquarters in the early 1990s and confidently announced that he was there for a job, he fully expected them to hire him on the spot. And they did. Most likely, it was his air of expectation that made it happen.

Finish Well – Remember "The Tortoise and the Hare?" The pokey old tortoise wins the race simply because he perseveres to the end.

A shooting star is impressive as it streaks across the night sky, but it's the reliable old sun shining on us that makes our survival possible. Wouldn't you rather be a dependable giver of life than just a beauty that runs too hot and fast and quickly burns out?

What I love and respect most about the Adams men – Horace, Buford, and Beau – is that they've reliably served Community Bible Church for the greater part of their lives, and in fifty years of ministry, there has never been even a hint of scandal from these men. That's finishing well.

Give – The best way to get what you want is to help others get what they want. Do you want love? Give it to yourself and offer it to others, and very quickly, you'll find you have all the love you can stand. Do you want respect? Be respectful. Do you want success? Help others be successful, and be happy even when your competitors succeed (after all, it means that there truly is a market for what you're doing!). Do you want more money? Give a portion of your income away with no strings attached.

God promises to multiply what you give and then send it back to you. "Give, and it will be given to you. A good measure, pressed down, shaken together and running over, will be poured into your lap. For with the measure you use, it will be measured to you" (Luke 6:38, NIV).

Many years ago, the church's leadership committed to giving a percentage of its income to missions. It's one of the reasons the church has weathered several recessions and has experienced fifty years of sustained financial stability in a "business" that has just as many failures as successes.

Be Happy – The wisest man who ever lived, King Solomon, said, "I know that there is nothing better for people than to be happy and to do good while they live. That each of them may eat and drink, and find satisfaction in all their toil—this is the gift of God" (Ecclesiastes 3:12-13, NIV).

God wants us to be happy. It's the goal of all other goals, and the search for it is the reason for most everything we do. The conditions we put on our happiness are what make it so elusive. We decide we'll only be happy if we marry the right person or if our kids behave or if the dog doesn't chew on the legs of the new coffee table. We delay happiness by promising ourselves a ROUND TUIT – *I'll be happy when this or that finally happens.* Happiness is a matter of stringing together happy moments, and we miss the happy moments while we're searching for the right conditions under which we're willing to be happy. What if we removed the conditions and simply decided to be happy no matter what happens?

The point of church is to stop our searching for God by realizing that He is always already right here right now. The same is true of happiness. Put no conditions on your happiness, and you'll find that you already have it. And God will be waiting for you right there in the middle of that happiness.

Love Learning --- In an old Hindu legend about Saraswati and Lakshmi, the goddesses of knowledge and wealth, a young man asks his teacher the secret to obtaining great wealth. The teacher tells him that Lakshmi (wealth) is jealous, and if the young man pays more attention to Saraswati (knowledge), then Lakshmi (wealth) will pursue him.

The church has always been open to helping its pastors pay for continuing education. It is a policy that can only help the ministry, and a similar attitude, that education is always worth the price, is a good one to adopt in our own lives. In recent years, the cost of higher education has skyrocketed, and for the first time in the history of our country, people are graduating from college and wondering if they will ever make enough money to pay for that expensive education. This is a shame, of course, but in a way, it's helping bring us back to the idea that an education is a privilege and not a right. That attitude can only serve to make us hungry for knowledge and more grateful for any chance we have to learn.

Proverbs 1:5-7 says, "A wise man will hear and increase in learning, and a man of understanding will acquire wise counsel to understand a proverb and a figure. . . . The fear of the Lord is the beginning of knowledge; fools despise wisdom and instruction" (NASB).

Don't be a fool. Even if you've earned the highest degree of formal education possible, find ways to keep learning.

Express Gratitude -- In the many boxes of church records from the past fifty years, there are several files filled with copies of Buford's correspondence. The vast majority of those letters are thank you letters.

Gratitude is powerful. It generates good will in the giver, making him or her more open to continued generosity, for we are much more willing to keep giving when our efforts are acknowledged and appreciated. But an attitude of gratitude also changes the person who expresses it. Appreciation for everything that shows up in our lives is a way of demonstrating to God that we're ready for bigger and better blessings.

Welcome Everyone – If you were to ask those first few teenagers who showed up at the Atlanta Youth Ranch in 1965 what attracted them, they'll most likely answer, "The swimming pool," or "A cute girl invited me." But when pressed to give a reason for why they went back the next week and the week after that, the answer will be that they felt like they belonged. Buford made it the ministry's mission to make sure every kid who walked through the doors was greeted enthusiastically and welcomed without hesitation. That focus has never changed. From the time *Cheers* became a hit television show in the 1980s, Buford has quoted these lines from its theme song, "You wanna go where people know, people are all the same, You wanna go where everybody knows your name." Realizing that, on some level, we are all the same naturally leads to accepting and loving everyone (even ourselves!), and that is the only way to be attractive, both personally and as a ministry.

My thanks and deepest appreciation to these people for providing quick answers to my questions about certain aspects of the church's history: Arlene Mlynczyk, Steve Shivers, Arnette Swift, Kim Johnson Norton, Alan Parker, Kent Kelso, Sammy Benton, Vince Pinyard, Peggy Evans, Joy Clemons, Paula Brannon, Amie Berry Rush, Harry Pittman, Horace Adams, Holly Adams, and Gerry and Donna Adams.

Brad Ellis spent a good hour outlining the beginnings of the contemporary service. Toney Jones told me his story. Jack Bartlett sat down for two different interviews, allowed me to pester him with questions for the better part of three years, and tracked down most of the photos in this book.

Glenn Hall created the sound track for this book's trailer, and his wife, Cindy, tracked down several of the pictures for it.

Dannie Chastain graciously provided the lyrics to "Friends in Both Places."

Karen Masters and Deborah Arnold found people to answer to my questions, located more photos, and helped me in many other ways.

And, of course, my mom, dad, and brother patiently answered questions – sometimes, the same question more than once because I'd misplaced my notes – during the three years I researched and wrote this book.

Finally, I want to express my everlasting gratitude to my test readers, who saved me from certain embarrassment -- Jack Bartlett, Kim Adams, Jenine Holmes, Carrie Bistline, Darlyn Finch Kuhn, Cathy Randall, and the Spalding University Spring 2012 Creative Nonfiction workshop (Bill Goodman, Martha Bourlakas, Cathy Conway Slider, Cheryl Butler Brandreth, Diane Aprile, Roy Hoffman, Sherry Palmer, Nicole La Chica, Issac Stolzenbach, and Anjila Joi Gaudet).

One final note: as this book was going to press, Horace Adams suffered a heart attack and a stroke. After a few days in the hospital and rehab, he moved into an assisted living facility in Henry County, where he is receiving excellent attention and loving care. Still, the transition has been difficult for him. Please keep him in your prayers.

Sources:

Burns, Rebecca. *Burial for a King*. New York: Scribner, 2011. Print.

Kundell, James E. "Status of Georgia Wetlands Policies and Procedures."
Proceedings of the 1993 Georgia Water Resources Conference.
<https://smartech.gatech.edu/bitstream/handle/1853/33101/ KundellJ2-93.pdf;jsessionid=63BA817074DDFDB53F453EC1AF 1BEBA4.smart1?sequence=1>.

Lee, Chris. "The Sex Addiction Epidemic." *Newsweek*. 25 November 2011.
http://www.newsweek.com/sex-addiction-epidemic-66289

Newman, Harvey K. *The Atlanta Housing Authority's Olympic Legacy Program: Public Housing Projects to Mixed-Income Communities.*
Atlanta: GSU Press. 2002. Print

Stetzer, Ed. "Learning from America's Largest and Fastest-Growing Churches."
SermonCentral.com. Web.

Wheatley, Thomas. "Clayton County's Tribulations." *Creative Loafing*. 23 July 2008.